INSTANT LESSONS

FOR SUPPLY TEACHERS

Candy Adler

7-9

YEARS

A & C Black • London

Dedicated to my Mum who would have been so proud!

I would like to personally thank the following people for their contributions to this book in one way or another:
My son Lee; my lovely Dad, Arnie, and Gill; Pat Woodcock-Howes; Sharon Laming – la mia amica bella and her husband David; the very talented Katie Collins; Deputy Head and teacher extraordinaire, Koula Christofides-Quinn; the dynamic Alan Cocker and all the staff and children at Cranborne Primary School, Potters Bar, Herts; Laura Schofield at Capita Education Resourcing (Luton branch); Dawn King; Lindsey White; Michelle Collins; Bob, Mandy and Alan at the Cock o' the North, Bell Bar, Herts for all the cappuccini, backchat, laughter, encouragement and allowing me to spread my work all over the table; everyone else who has helped me along the way.

Published 2009 by A & C Black Publishers Limited
36 Soho Square, London W1D 3QY
www.acblack.com

ISBN 978-1-4081-1158-1

Copyright text: © Candy Adler 2009
Copyright illustrations: © Catherine Ward 2009
Copyright cover illustration: © KJA Artists 2009
Editor: Margot O'Keeffe
Designed by: Blade Communications
CD-ROM designed and developed by Cambridge Digital (www.cambridgedigital.com); produced by Will Burrows

A CIP catalogue record for this book is available from the British Library.

The author and publishers gratefully acknowledge permission to reproduce the following copyright material:

Shutterstock for:
Design a Savannah Grassland Animal Resource Sheets 1 and 2: Giraffe (25328587) Peter Betts; Savannah elephant (21256609) Isaiah Shook; Cheetah (25915756) Nickolay Stanev; Warthog (14802553) Anke van Wyk

Map Symbols Resource Sheet 1: Wheelchair access symbol (10801480) WilleeCole; Ladies & Gents (25880410) PixelShow

Design a Stained-Glass Window Resource Sheet: Sun in sky (1190911) photobank ch; Grapes (2954056) Mary Terriberry; Blue window (3528368) Nolie; Butterfly – square (11665381) Ivan Ulybyshev; Circular butterflies (13980217) tasha_chu; Tiger (16703491) Steffen Foerster Photography; Pattern arch (17155885) Toponium; Triptych (19823725) sahua d; Pattern circular (20085976) sokolovsky.

Design a Coat of Arms Resource Sheet 1: Recycling symbol (26329555) Pakhnyushcha; Wheelchair access symbol (10801480) WilleeCole; No cycling symbol

(19667614) Anton Novik; For sale sign (25030423) Feverpitch; Tick and cross (24481924) Alex Mit; Ladies & Gents (25880410) PixelShow; Pound sign (25320397) Georgios Kollidas; Stop sign (21549514) Christophe Testi.

Design a Coat of Arms Resource Sheet 2: Castle (23555359) Klara Viskova; Flag (1651350) John Rawsterne; Corgi (331351) Patricia Marroquin; Crown (19461502) Mushakesa.

Taking a Line For a Walk: Image by Paul Friedlander www.paulfriedlander.com

Musical Moods: Pennsylvania 6-5000 Glenn Miller Orchestra (RCA)/Three of a Kind - Kenny G (Arista)] Courtesy of Sony Music Entertainment Inc Licensed by Sony Music Commercial Markets UK

Vivaldi – Spring Dance: Cavendish Music (Publisher) for THE FOUR SEASONS by Vivaldi (Composer): Spring (Allegro)

Every effort has been made to trace copyright holders and to obtain their permission for use of copyright material. The author and publishers would be pleased to rectify any error or omission in future editions.

Printed and bound in India by Replika Press Pvt. Ltd.

10 9 8 7 6 5 4 3 2

A & C Black uses paper produced with elemental chlorine-free pulp, harvested from managed sustainable forests.

Contents

Instant Lessons for Supply Teachers

The job of the supply teacher is one of the most challenging in education. Supply teachers are expected, at short notice, to enter a classroom full of unfamiliar pupils and to deliver inclusive lessons that take account of pupils with differing abilities and that engage them all in worthwhile, curriculum-relevant learning experiences.

The *Instant Lessons for Supply Teachers* series offers a bank of lesson plans and reproducible resources across the curriculum, which can be used at a moment's notice by teachers providing emergency cover. There are three books, one each for 5–7 year olds, 7–9 year olds and 9–11 year olds. Each of these provides 30 lesson plans – 10 Literacy, 10 Mathematics and 10 spread across the other areas of learning (Science, History, Geography, Art, Design, Music, PE and PSHE).

Each book is accompanied by a CD-ROM with all the resources needed – ready-to-print, so there's no need to carry around multiple books and bulky materials. In addition, the CD-ROMs contain PowerPoint versions of all the lesson plans so they can be displayed for whole-class use on an interactive whiteboard.

About the books

Each book contains:
- An introduction explaining how the resources are organised.
- Practical tips and essential information for supply teachers.
- A lesson-plan for each of the 30 lessons. Each of these is presented in a unique and easy-to-use grid format.

The lessons are not numbered as it is not intended that they should be done in a specific order, but rather that they should be dipped into and chosen as appropriate to the needs of the class. It is envisaged that each lesson will take about one hour unless otherwise stated.

- One of the reproducible sheets that accompany the lesson, to give you a glimpse, as you read the lesson plan, of how the resources support the lesson. That sheet as well as all other sheets can be found on the CD-ROM.

- Answers, as appropriate, to lesson-plan activities.

Overview of the CD-ROMs

For each lesson in the book, the CD-ROM contains:

- A PowerPoint presentation of the lesson plan for using on an interactive whiteboard
- The Lesson-Plan Grid
- A list of Success Criteria
- Reproducible and customisable Resource and Activity Sheets
- Where appropriate, colour Resource Sheets for display on an interactive whiteboard
- For some lessons (e.g. Music, PE/Dance), audio files of music
- Some Generic Resources for general use within the Maths section
- The pages of this book as a PDF for viewing and printing out.

For further information, please see page 6 'How to use the CD-ROM'.

Sample lesson-plan grid

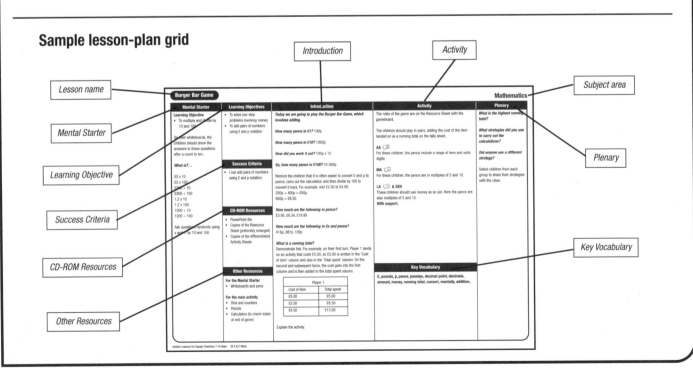

The lesson-plan grids (see facing page)

Each grid provides:

- Learning Objective/s
- Success Criteria
- A list of the CD-ROM Resources required
- A list of Other Resources required
- An Introduction to the lesson, to be used with the whole class
- Description of the group, paired or individual Activity for different levels of ability
- A Key Vocabulary word bank
- Ideas for a Plenary session

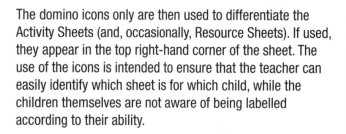

In addition:

- All Mathematics lesson-plan grids have a Mental Starter section.
- All Literacy lesson-plan grids in *Instant Lessons for Supply Teachers 5-7 Years* have a Phonics Starter section.

Differentiation

Where relevant, ideas are provided for differentiating the content of the lesson to suit the needs of the different abilities in a class. When differentiation by task is suggested, the notes in the Activity section of the lesson-plan grid are organised under the following headings with accompanying domino icons:

AA

The suggestions here are for children with an above average ability, or at the top end of the book's age range.

MA

The suggestions here are for children of average ability, or in the middle of the book's age range.

LA

The suggestions here are for children of lower ability, or at the lower end of the book's age range.

SEN

Usually the children with Special Education Needs are given the same task as the LA children. However, occasionally added support for these children is necessary.

The domino icons only are then used to differentiate the Activity Sheets (and, occasionally, Resource Sheets). If used, they appear in the top right-hand corner of the sheet. The use of the icons is intended to ensure that the teacher can easily identify which sheet is for which child, while the children themselves are not aware of being labelled according to their ability.

The reproducible sheets

Activity Sheets

Activity Sheets are those sheets on which the children will be inputting information in some form. This may be writing, completing tables or creating designs and artwork. These sheets are differentiated where possible and this is shown using the dominoes icons described above.

Support Activity Sheets

These sheets are for children who need additional support.

Resource Sheets

Resource Sheets are non-consumable sheets. They are not intended for the children to write on. It is recommended that they are displayed on the whiteboard or enlarged copies printed out and displayed somewhere in the classroom. In some cases, these are provided in full colour. Many of the Resource Sheets are gameboards. In some cases, they are also differentiated so that the children play the game most suited to their ability, even though it has the same objective as the other gameboard(s) for other ability groups. Again, these could be enlarged and laminated. In some cases, the rules are on the gameboard itself and, in other cases, the rules are a separate Resource Sheet to be displayed or for the children to keep with them. It is recommended that you explain or read through any game rules with the children; the reading level of the written rules may not be accessible to all children.

Generic Sheets

The CD-ROM contains a collection of Generic Sheets within the Maths section:

- Number lines: 0–100, 0–50 and 0–20
- Playing cards for the numbers 1 to 10
- Playing cards for the numbers 11 to 20
- Playing cards for the numbers 21 to 30
- Multiplication squares
- 100 squares
- Numbers Word Bank

It would be useful to have these laminated so that they can be used many times, rather than printing off several sheets.

Supply Teacher Feedback Form

The Supply Teacher Feedback Form on page 72 (and also on the CD-ROM) provides a helpful template on which to feed back information to the class teacher. A filled-in exemplar is provided on page 73 of this book.

Answers

Answers to activities are provided as appropriate, both at the back of this book (on pages 74–80) and on the CD-ROM along with the other resources for the relevant lesson unit.

The PowerPoint presentations

The PowerPoint presentations offer you an alternative method of delivering the lesson. As you talk the class through the various points, a frame-by-frame version of the lesson, together with any diagrams or sample sheets needed to demonstrate the activity, is displayed.

You can move down the points by clicking on the screen or using the page down key on the keyboard. Note that a small red + sign indicates that there is more text to follow on that slide.

The Success Criteria sheet features towards the end of the presentation – before the Plenary session – so that it can be left on display for the children to refer to as they work.

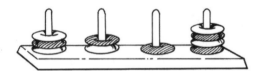

How to use the CD-ROM

The CD-ROM included with this book contains an easy-to-use interface that allows to you to print out pages from the book, to view them (e.g. on an interactive whiteboard) or to customise the activities to suit the needs of your pupils.

Getting started

Insert the CD-ROM into your CD drive and the disk should autorun and launch the interface in your web browser. If the disk does not autorun, open 'My Computer' and select the CD drive, then open the file 'start.exe'. If you are using a Mac, select the CD drive and open the 'start.app' file.

Please note: due to the differences between Mac and PC fonts, you may experience some unavoidable variations in typography and page layouts.

Navigating through the CD-ROM

The Home Screen provides links to the following areas of the CD-ROM: the End User Licence Agreement, the Supply Teacher Feedback Form, and the main menu or Contents Page.

Four options are available to you from the Contents page:

1. The first option takes you to the Book PDF, where you can choose pages of the book to view and print out, using Adobe Reader (see below).

2. The second option takes you to the Mathematics lessons resources.

3. The third option takes you to the Literacy lessons resources.

4. The fourth option takes you to the Other Subjects lessons resources.

Click on any of options 2–4 to display a list of the 10 lessons in the relevant section. Then click on a lesson title to display all the resources for that lesson.

There is a 'Back' button in the top right of the Contents screen to return to the Home Screen.

If you do not have the Microsoft Office suite (with Word and PowerPoint), you might like to consider using OpenOffice instead. This is a multi-platform and multilingual office suite, and an 'open-source' project. It is compatible with all other major office suites, and the product is free to download, use and distribute (see www.openoffice.org). Other compatible software includes Ability Office and Star Office. Use an Internet search engine to locate current versions of alternative software.

If you do not already have Adobe Reader (for accessing PDF files) it can be downloaded for free from www.adobe.com.

File formats

You will find four different file formats on the CD-ROM:

- PowerPoint files (PPT) enabling the lessons to be presented on an interactive whiteboard;

- MP3 files containing music tracks for Music and PE/Dance lessons*;

- PDF files of all resources enabling them to be viewed, displayed on an interactive whiteboard or visualiser, and printed;

- WORD files of many of the resources, enabling you to edit and customise the resource – and to print it out, or copy and paste it into your existing planning using Microsoft Word.

*NB: This CD-ROM cannot be used in a CD player. The audio tracks on the CD-ROM are provided in mp3 format. These can be copied from CD or computer onto a media player such as an mp3 player, or copied to a new CD to use in a CD player for personal or educational use. No rights of distribution are granted or implied by this.

Technical support

If you have any question regarding the *Instant Lessons for Supply Teachers* software, please email us at the address below. We will get back to you as quickly as possible.

educationalsales@acblack.com

Example Lesson Resources: Cutting Compound Words

The following is an example of a lesson with the recources provided.

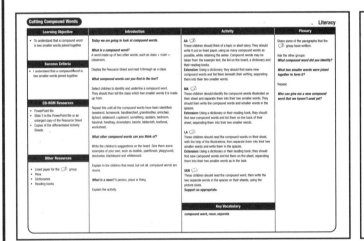

Lesson Plan Grid

Success Criteria

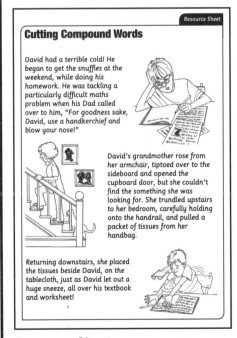

Resource Sheet

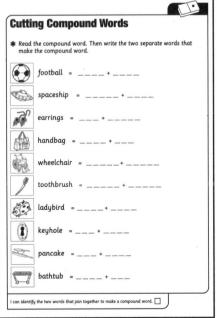

Activity Sheet

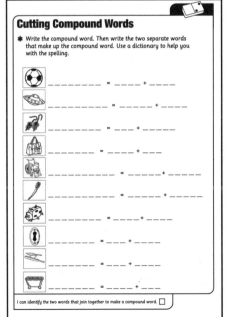

Activity Sheet

Getting Started

Types of supply-teaching work

There are generally three different types of supply-teaching work available:

- Day-to-day work involves covering sickness, training courses, conferences and so on. In the case of sickness, this type of work usually involves last-minute, early-morning calls. Cover for conferences and training courses is most often pre-booked.

- Longer-term work may involve any cover from a week to a half term (6-8 weeks).

- Fixed contract may involve cover for between a half term to an academic year – to cover long-term sickness, maternity leave and so on.

Ways of getting supply work

Local Education Authority (LEA)

To obtain supply teaching work through your Local Education Authority, you must register with them. The procedure will differ from LEA to LEA. If your work comes via an LEA, you should be paid to scale and have pension options through your relevant county. Payment is usually made through their own payroll. Rules of employment vary between LEAs, so check with whichever covers the areas in which you wish to work for their individual conditions and rules.

Agencies

Before registering with an agency, it is valuable to seek recommendations. Talking to other supply teachers is a good place to start. Additionally, schools often have a favourite agency to which they are loyal, so if you wish to work in particular schools, try to find out which agencies they use. You might wish to register with several in order to get sufficient work. However, be aware that agencies set their own rates of pay and this is usually less than LEAs.

Directly through schools

You can only be employed by a school if you already have an LEA payroll number which requires registration with the LEA.

In all cases, you will need to have a Criminal Records Bureau (CRB) Disclosure form. The LEA, agency or school should be able to advise you on obtaining and completing the form.

Preparation

What do I take to school with me?

- ✔ This book and the accompanying CD-ROM
- ✔ A project file containing hard copies from the CD-ROM of relevant lesson plans, Resource Sheets and Activity Sheets
- ✔ Your CRB form, a photo ID card if you have one and your GTC registration card
- ✔ Bottled water (This is sometimes charged for, as are hot drinks. You should offer to pay for any refreshments you have.)
- ✔ Lunch (although it is often possible to order and purchase a lunch if you do it by break time)
- ✔ A story or poetry book (as a filler or for the end of the day)
- ✔ Coloured pens (check the school's policy on marking the register and children's work)
- ✔ Sticky tack (for the Success Criteria and other display material)
- ✔ Counters and dice for the games
- ✔ Trainers to change into if you have to take a PE lesson
- ✔ A small book to keep details of lesson times, names of the Headteacher and other staff and any other relevant notes for future visits
- ✔ Stickers as a reward for good work or behaviour
- ✔ Timesheet – without it you won't get paid!

When should I arrive?

If you say you are available for work, you should be up and ready to go. Schools really appreciate your arriving early, so estimate how long it will take you to get there and be sure to plan your route. Being prepared before the children arrive is paramount to a successful first impression. Ideally you should aim to arrive at least 30 minutes before the start of school.

What should I wear?

Dress professionally, but comfortably. There is an unwritten dress code, which means that jeans and track suits are not acceptable, unless, of course, you are given prior permission to wear these for PE. Wear footwear that you can take PE in or take trainers with you to change into. If you are female, avoid low necklines and short skirts.

What do I do when I get there?

Not all of the following issues need to be addressed as soon as you arrive. However, if you are able to get there early enough to do so, it will make life a lot easier!

- You will have to sign the visitor's book and offer your CRB and identification.
- You may or may not be shown the staff room and the toilets – if not, ask.
- Check whether there is an interactive whiteboard (IWB) in your classroom. If yes, check that it is connected to a laptop or computer and that it is working. If not, you will need hard copies of everything you need for your lessons.
- Find the timetable. Often there is a copy on the wall for the children. This will tell you what the routines are and what time things like assembly are. You should assume you are to attend.
- Fire drill instructions are usually displayed. Make sure you know where the meeting point is.

If you are not told, ask:

- whether you are on break duty – if the class teacher for whom you are covering is on duty, you will probably be expected to do their duty (a list is usually on a board in the staffroom);
- if you stay in the classroom during wet play or will be relieved;
- whether any planning has been left for you (if it has, read it through so that if there are any problems, you have time to query it and/or use the photocopier);
- whether there are any children of whom you need to be especially aware (e.g. those with SENs or behaviour problems);
- what the school behaviour policy is so that you know how to react to bad behaviour;
- whether there is a bell to indicate the end of morning sessions;
- whether or not you collect the class in the morning/breaks and so on, and if so, from where;
- whether or not you lead children out at the end of the day or wait for parents to collect them.

Many classrooms have a Teaching Assistant (TA) assigned to them for at least part of the day. They are a valuable resource, so use them! Not only will they support your teaching, but they are also a treasure trove of information with regard to the individual children, ability groups, the class, school routines and rules, and, very importantly, where the resources are kept. (Be aware: headteachers often ask teaching assistants for feedback about you!)

What will the school expect of me?

Schools expect a supply teacher who will provide professional teaching cover with the minimum disruption to the class and school routine. If work has been left by the class teacher, then it must be taught. However, there may be occasions where you are unable to do so due to lack of resources required or understanding of the planning. In these incidences, use your own lesson plans, but ensure you note your reasons for doing so and what you taught instead on your feedback form.

In addition to effective teaching, schools will also expect you to:

- be prepared and adaptable – things change rapidly in a school day;
- have good control of the class;
- mark all work taught (see 'Marking', page 11);
- leave feedback for the class teacher (see Feedback Form, page 72);
- leave the classroom tidy, shut all windows and turn off lights, computers and the IWB projector;
- report to the office to have your timesheet signed, and sign out.

Behaviour management

Behaviour management is one of the biggest issues in primary classrooms today. You probably have your own strategies that are tried and tested, and that you use on a day-to-day basis. However, we all have different natures and teaching styles, and every catchment area is slightly different, as is every class temperament. What works with some classes or teachers won't necessarily work with others. You need to be adaptable and try different tactics until you find what works for both you and the individual class. The most important thing to remember, however frustrated or exasperated you may feel, is not to lose your temper or shout. Not only will this not result in effective class control, it is likely to exacerbate the situation, causing more problems.

If you don't enjoy teaching in a school because of continued bad behaviour, you don't need to go back. However, you should see any day through to the end. If it is really bad, then there is nothing wrong with asking for help. Other members of staff will usually be willing to offer advice, recognising that it is more difficult to control the behaviour of children you don't know.

First impressions

Children don't like changes to their routines. They need to feel safe and relaxed to be ready to learn. Show that you are in control but approachable. Preparation is the key. Have some early morning work on the board for when they enter the classroom, to keep them occupied while you are dealing with the inevitable queries and issues that arise first thing. Write the date, 'Good morning' and 'My name is …'. Beneath this write the task; for example, 'How many small words can you make out of this word: impossible?' Other tasks might be practising spellings/tables or writing as many number sentences as possible for a chosen number (choose according to ability).

Establishing your expectations from the outset

- Smile but be authoritative when you speak.
- Select sensible children to help you with any important morning jobs, such as taking the register to the office.
- Appoint a helper of the day.
- Lay down your main class rules as soon as possible and give the children a clear idea of your expectations for the day.
- Request silence for the register, and ask the children to respond to their name by answering and giving a little wave so that you can put a face to the name.

Making it personal

The sooner you know the children's names, the better. This puts them at ease and helps with class control. Try giving each child a sticky label with their name on it to wear. Your teaching assistant may be able to find the sticky labels and do this for you. Or you can carry some in your supply kit, just in case. Alternatively, you could give the children an A4 sheet of paper to fold horizontally and write their first names in large, clear letters so that you can see it from the front of the class.

Putting them at their ease

We all like to know what we are likely to be doing for the day, so tell the children what you have planned. Try to praise them often as possible. Comment on how patiently children are sitting or waiting to speak and acknowledge the efforts some children make in trying to answer a question even if the answer is wrong. Good behaviour that is being noticed and rewarded can be contagious!

Remember to give the children 'settling in' time. Many of them will try to test you. Equally, many children will be very wary of you; after all, you are an 'unknown quantity'.

Children with special needs

Special needs may range from ADHD to dyslexia, dyspraxia, autism and learning difficulties. The

Headteacher or other staff will usually make a point of providing you with information on such children. These children will need activities that are related to what the other children in the class are doing but at their ability level so they can achieve success like everyone else. If their needs are very different, there is usually a Learning Support Assistant (LSA) to support them. They can be a great help in adapting your suggested activities. By all means give special needs children jobs to boost their self-esteem, but sometimes it is just giving them the correct level of work that can produce the best behaviour, especially if it is really interesting to them.

Sanctions

Be aware of the school's behaviour and sanctions policy. Don't make threats you can't carry out or the children will not take the threat seriously next time. Make sure that the children know your expectations regarding behaviour and aim to keep them high but in a positive way.

Stop, look and listen

Children like to chat when they are supposed to be working and the noise level in a classroom needs to remain at a workable level. If a teacher becomes louder to make her/himself heard, the children tend to get louder still. Shouting (unless you have a reason to be very angry) is never successful.

Some useful strategies are:
- Say quietly 'If you can hear me, put your hand on your head'. It is surprising how quickly the class catches on!
- Try touching your head, then shoulders and so on. Children are quick to copy you, thereby helping you to gain whole-class attention in a short time.
- Use an instrument, such as a shaker, tambourine or little drum, to catch the class' attention.
- Try using signs: for example, an ear for 'listen', a red traffic light for 'stop talking', dimming or turning the lights on or off to get children's attention.
- Standing with arms folded, exaggeratedly looking at the clock or watch, until silence prevails can take quite a while, but it does work.
- Use a timer, counting up. Explain, 'If you waste my time, I'll waste yours. This is coming out of your break/lunchtime.' It is amazing how quickly it works. Always give them a chance to earn the time back!

Explain activities and keep children on task

It is important to position yourself in the classroom so that all the children can see you (and you them). When explaining a task, ask several children to repeat it. Be aware that some children with special educational needs might need instructions simplified and given one at a time. They may not be able to remember a list.

Set a time limit in which to complete work. Again, the timer could be used for this. If you are not working with a particular group, circulate around the classroom, commenting on good work or application, and helping where needed. If children have their hands up for help and you are already helping someone, tell them to ask their study partner/work buddy/person sitting next to them for help, and that you will be over shortly.

Serious incidents

Any serious incidents should be reported to the Headteacher or Deputy Head, whether they be behavioural or something a child has disclosed to you in confidence. In the case of the latter, do not encourage the child by asking questions and do not, under any circumstances, show a reaction or promise not to tell anyone else.

Do not restrain fighting children. Try blowing a whistle to shock them to attention, and send another child for help, according to the school policy, in order to protect yourself from allegations and from injuries. In the case of a child who is behaving in a way that might endanger any of the children, act in accordance with the school policy. In the absence of that, usher the rest of the class out to the nearest classroom. Under no circumstances should you make any bodily contact with a child when reprimanding them. This could be interpreted as assault, even if you have only touched their arm.

Safety issues

In order to keep the children and yourself safe while working in a school, remember:

- to be familiar with and follow the school guidelines if there is a fire;

- to follow safety guidelines during P.E. lessons – for example, children should:
    - remove all jewellery and cover any earrings that cannot be removed;
    - wear shoes when walking to and from the hall;

- not to give the children anything to eat or drink of your own.

Assessment

A supply teacher undertaking long-term cover is likely to have been given the class teacher's planning to follow and will be expected to carry out more detailed assessments. The lessons in this book are intended for use when doing varied daily supply teaching, so the only assessment will be during the lesson with questioning and marking the work.

Assessment for learning, or formative assessment, is diagnostic, usually oral, through asking questions and discussion. It is already present in the lesson plans in this book in the form of key questions within the Introduction and Plenary sessions. As you circulate, ask children specific questions about their work, for example: How did you know that? How did you get that answer? How did you work that out? What strategy did you use? Why do you think that is? What do you think you need to do next?

Don't forget to praise and give constructive feedback to move the children forward in order that they make progress.

Assessment of learning, or summative assessment, will be carried out primarily through marking. The 'I can…' success-criteria statements at the bottom of most Activity Sheets are intended for children to complete themselves to support self-assessment.

Marking

All work must be marked – it is part of your job and is usually incorporated into the contract you signed. Marking must be finished before you leave the class.

All schools have a marking policy, often displayed on the wall for the children. A glance through the books will tell you how the teacher marks and in what colour. Only mark to the learning objective set. If it is to write rhyming couplets and the couplets don't rhyme, then the learning objective has clearly not been achieved. You may wish to correct a few of the most commonly misspelled words. Maths and literacy should include a comment to help the children improve. For example, if, when marking angles, the child has not used the degrees symbol, you could write: 'Good work, X, but remember to use the symbol for degrees – °.'

What do I do at the end of the day?

✔ Leave time at the end of the day so that the children can clear up.

✔ Ask the children whether they stack the chairs, put them up on the tables or leave them.

✔ Complete any marking.

✔ Fill in the Feedback Form (see page 72).

✔ Check that the computers and projector are turned off, close the windows and turn out the lights.

✔ Get your timesheet signed, sign out and, if appropriate, give some verbal feedback to the Headteacher or secretary.

Tables: What's My Question?

Mental Starter	Learning Objectives	Introduction	Activity	Plenary
Learning Objective • To recall multiplication facts for the 3, 5, 6 and 10 times tables Play Fizz Buzz. Go round the class counting on in multiples of 3. If the number is a multiple of 3, the child should say 'Fizz' and if a multiple of 5, they should say 'Buzz'. If it is a multiple of both, such as 15, they should say 'Fizz Buzz'. Repeat this for multiples of 6: 'Fizz' if a multiple of 6, 'Buzz' if a multiple of 10 and 'Fizz Buzz' if a multiple of both.	• To recall multiplication facts to 10 x 10 • To find the factors for a product **Success Criteria** • I can recall the facts of the 2, 3, 4, 5, 6 and 10 tables. • I can find the factors for a product. **CD-ROM Resources** • PowerPoint file • Slide 9 in the PowerPoint file or an enlarged copy of Generic Sheet 5 (10 x 10 multiplication squares) • Slide 11 in the PowerPoint file or an enlarged copy of the Activity Sheet • Copies of the differentiated Activity Sheets • Copies of Generic Sheet 5 • Answers Sheet **Other Resources** • Multi-link cubes or similar for SEN children	*Today we are going to practise our tables by looking at the answers in a tables puzzle and writing the questions.* *What does 'product' mean?* The answer when two numbers are multiplied together. *Does anyone know what we call the two numbers that are multiplied together?* Factors. Reiterate that when we multiply two factors (numbers) together, we get a product. Write on the board: $3 \times 4 = 12$ factors product Discuss using facts the children know, such as '6 is double 3', '4 is double 2' and '4 is half of 8'. Remind them that with multiplication calculations (as with addition) you can change the order of the factors (unlike with subtraction and division). For example, $3 \times 4 = 12$ and $4 \times 3 = 12$. *Can you give me a pair of factors (numbers that you multiply together) for the following products:* *12?* $2 \times 6, 6 \times 2, 3 \times 4, 4 \times 3$ *18?* $2 \times 9, 9 \times 2, 3 \times 6, 6 \times 3$ *24?* $3 \times 8, 8 \times 3, 4 \times 6, 6 \times 4$ *How can we use a multiplication square to help us find factors if we can't recall our times tables?* Display Generic Sheet 5 and show the children how to use the multiplication square. Explain the activity. **NB:** It is likely that many children will not have done a crossword-style puzzle, so you will need to explain the across and down numbering system.	**AA** These children should look at the completed puzzle and write multiplication questions for each answer, recalling facts for all the times tables to 10, in particular 7, 8 and 9. **MA** These children should look at the completed puzzle and write the multiplication questions for each answer, recalling facts for the 2, 3, 4, 5, 6 and 10 times tables. **LA** These children should look at the completed puzzle and write multiplication questions for each answer, recalling multiplication facts for the 2, 3, 4, 5, 6 and 10 times tables, using a multiplication square for support where appropriate. **SEN with support** The LSA should choose the 2, 3 or 4 times table, whichever is appropriate. Ask the child to count on in 2s, using multi-link cubes, saying, '1 lot of 2 is 2', placing two cubes in a horizontal line. '2 lots of 2 is 4', then counting out and placing 4 cubes beneath the 2, in pairs and so on. Repeat this for 3s, then 4s. **Key Vocabulary** **multiple, product, factors, numbers, multiply, multiplication, double, half, strategy, inverse, divide, division, answer**	If appropriate, the children can swap their work and peer mark with a coloured pencil, using a multiplication square to check. They can then swap back and reflect on any questions they got wrong. Explain that this exercise shows up the areas they need to concentrate on. Alternatively, show the puzzle and point to an answer. *Who can give me a question for this answer?* Repeat.

Tables: What's My Question?

✳ Look at the puzzle answers. For each one, write one possible question in the Across and Down grids.

	Across	
1	X	=
3	X	=
5	X	=
9	X	=
10	X	=
11	X	=
14	X	=
16	X	=
17	X	=
19	X	=
21	X	=
22	X	=
24	X	=
25	X	=
27	X	=
30	X	=
31	X	=
33	X	=
34	X	=
36	X	=
38	X	=
39	X	=
40	X	=

Puzzle grid

1 4	2 9		3 1	4 8		5 6	6 4			7 7
8 2			9 2	1		10 3	5			2
	11 5	4			12 2			13 6		
14 5	6		15 2		16 8	1		17 3	18 6	
0		19 2	4			20 3			4	
	21 4	8		22 1	23 5		24 2	0		
25 4	2		26 3		27 6	28 3			29 4	
8		30 1	6			31 2	32 8		0	
	33 3	0		34 2	35 7		36 1	37 2		
38 4	5				39 2	4		40 5	4	

	Down	
1	X	=
3	X	=
4	X	=
5	X	=
6	X	=
7	X	=
11	X	=
12	X	=
13	X	=
14	X	=
15	X	=
18	X	=
19	X	=
20	X	=
21	X	=
23	X	=
25	X	=
26	X	=
28	X	=
29	X	=
30	X	=
32	X	=
33	X	=
35	X	=
37	X	=

I can recall multiplication facts to 10 x 10, in particular 7, 8 and 9. ☐

Co-ordinates: Mirror My Pattern

Mental Starter	Learning Objective	Introduction	Activity	Plenary
Learning Objective • To use the eight compass points to describe direction Prepare by placing N, S, W and E signs in appropriate positions around the room. Point out North. *Where is South? West? East?* Draw a compass outline on the board. Add N, S, E and W. Remind or teach the children 'Naughty Elephants Squirt Water' or 'Never Eat Shredded Wheat'. Ask them to stand up and face the North sign in the classroom. *Face West. Face East.* Explain that they should turn clockwise each time. Now show or draw an eight-point compass on the board. N, S, W, E, NW, NE, SW, SE. Add these labels around the room in the correct places. Repeat the previous exercises using these additional points.	**Learning Objective** • To describe and identify the position of a square on a grid of squares **Success Criteria** • I can plot and read numeric co-ordinates. • I can plot and read alpha-numeric co-ordinates. **CD-ROM Resources** • PowerPoint file • Slide 7 in the PowerPoint file or an enlarged copy of the alpha-numeric grid • Activity Sheet • Copies of the differentiated Activity Sheets **Other Resources** **For the Mental Starter** • Large compass point signs • Sticky tack **For the main activity** • Pencils	*Today we are going to use our knowledge of the compass points and co-ordinates to play a game.* Draw an alpha-numeric grid on the board and colour in one square. (If using the grid in the PowerPoint file, point to the square.) Explain that, when using co-ordinates, we use 'Along the corridor and up the stairs' – the horizontal axis first and the vertical axis second. *What are the co-ordinates of this square?* Repeat this several times so that they understand how to read the co-ordinates. *Who can find these co-ordinates?* Give out several co-ordinates and invite individual children to colour the squares in on the board or point to them on the PowerPoint display. Starting with a new grid, point to or colour one square. *Where would you colour if I asked you to move from this square three squares East and one square South?* *What are the co-ordinates of the square you arrived at?* Invite the children to identify the square, colour it and identify the new co-ordinates. Explain that the correct way of writing co-ordinates is (3,4) or (A,2). Repeat this a few times. Show the children the enlarged ⬚ Activity Sheet with alpha-numeric grids. Explain how they should play the game. Demonstrate to the AA group how to use numeric co-ordinates instead of alpha-numeric ones.	Working in pairs, but with one Activity Sheet each, Child 1 should choose and secretly colour a square on the left grid (Mine). They tell their partner the co-ordinates, such as (4,3). Their partner should colour that square in on the grid on the right (My partner's) of their own sheet. Emphasise that they must write the co-ordinates of each square in the mirror as they colour it. They should compare grids with their partner to check they are both the same. If not, they should discuss where the mistake is. They should then swap over so the second child gives directions. **AA** ⬚ These children should use just the numeric co-ordinates. Remind them that the correct way to write co-ordinates is (2,4). They should identify the co-ordinates as requested. They could play the game in two teams but drawing simple shapes. **MA** ⬚ These children should use the alpha-numeric sheet and play the game in pairs. **LA** ⬚ **& SEN** These children should also play in pairs, using only alpha-numeric co-ordinates. **With support.** **Key Vocabulary** **direction, compass points, N, S, W, E, NW, NE, SW, SE, clockwise, horizontal, vertical, position, grid, co-ordinates, square, alpha-numeric, numeric, axis, x axis, y axis, axes**	Display a blank grid. Draw a simple pattern on a separate grid on a sheet of paper. Select children from different ability groups to come up, look at the pattern you have drawn and read out the co-ordinates for the pattern. Select other children to draw, on the displayed blank grid, the pattern according to the co-ordinates as they are read out. Finally, compare the drawn pattern with the one on the board.

Co-ordinates: Mirror My Pattern

Mine

6						
5						
4						
3						
2						
1						
	A	B	C	D	E	F

Co-ordinates

My partner's

6						
5						
4						
3						
2						
1						
	A	B	C	D	E	F

Co-ordinates

Mine

6						
5						
4						
3						
2						
1						
	A	B	C	D	E	F

Co-ordinates

My partner's

6						
5						
4						
3						
2						
1						
	A	B	C	D	E	F

Co-ordinates

I know how to plot and read alpha-numeric co-ordinates. □

Mental Starter

Learning Objective
- To make and describe right-angled turns, including turns between the four compass points

Explain that a ¼ turn is a right angle.

What is clockwise?

Establish where the compass points are. Starting by facing North (N), ask the children to then turn clockwise to East (E).

How many right angles have you turned?

Repeat this for S and W.

Starting at N, ask the children to turn clockwise to W.

How many right angles have you turned?

Repeat.

Learning Objectives

- To begin to know that angles are measured in degrees and that: one whole turn is 360° or four right angles; ¼ turn is 90° or one right angle; half a right angle is 45°

- To compare and measure angles less than 180° with set squares

Success Criteria

- I can compare and measure angles less than 180° with set squares.

CD-ROM Resources

- PowerPoint file
- Slide 7 in the PowerPoint file or an enlarged copy of the Resource Sheet
- Copies of the differentiated Activity Sheets
- Answers Sheet

Other Resources

- 90°, 45° and 90°, 60° and 30° set squares

Introduction

Today we are going to learn that angles are measured in degrees (°) and that a ¼ turn on a compass or clock face is 90°.

Write the degrees symbol on the board, the word 'degree' and then 90°. Ask the children which angles they already know. They should know the right angle, which is 90°.

Draw a square or rectangle on the board. ***How many 90° angles can you see?*** 4 ***So how many degrees does a square or rectangle have altogether?*** 4 x 90° = 360°

Remember our work on right-angled turns. A ¼ turn is the same as 90°. So ½ a turn (from N to W) is 180°. How many degrees are in a whole turn (from N back to N)? 360°

If you put 2 right angles together, how many degrees will it measure? 180°. Explain that this is a straight line.

Show them that half a right angle is 45°. Draw it on the board.

Display some angles (Resource Sheet). Point to them one at a time and ask questions about them.

Is this angle a right angle? Is this one bigger or smaller than a right angle?

Hold up some set squares. Explain that these are set squares and that we use them to measure angles. Look at a 45° set square. Explain that one angle is 90° and the other two are 45°. Then show them the 60° set square and explain that the angles are 90°, 60° and 30°.

Explain which part of the angle they should measure. Explain that angles are not always facing the same way.

Return to the Resource Sheet and use set squares to demonstrate how to measure the angles.

Explain the activity.

Activity

AA 📇

Working individually, these children should measure the angles on their sheet with set squares and label them with degrees. They should then answer the questions and order the angles.
Extension: They could draw some of their own angles using set squares and label them.

MA 📇

These children should work individually to measure the angles and compare them with a right angle. They should then find 2-D shapes in the classroom that have right angles and draw and label them, marking each right angle.

LA 📇

These children should work in pairs to compare the angles with a right angle. **Support as necessary.**
Extension: They could find examples of right angles in 2-D shapes in the classroom.

SEN

In a group, with support, these children should look for and identify right angles on objects within the classroom; for example, tables, books and windows, measuring them with their set squares to check. They can progress to 2-D shapes if they are available.
Extension: They could try the 📇 Activity Sheet.

Key Vocabulary

clockwise, anti-clockwise, rotate, whole turn, half turn, quarter turn, angles, right angle, degrees (°), set square, compare, measure

Plenary

Share the children's answers and correct any errors or misunderstandings.

Using a clock, move the hands and ask:

How many degrees has the minute hand moved?

Repeat this.

What shape do two right angles make? A straight line.

How many degrees in a whole turn?

Measuring Angles

✱ Measure each angle using the 45° and 60° set squares.
✱ In the box, write how many degrees it measures.

A

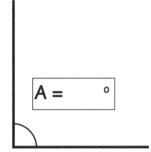

A = ____ °

B

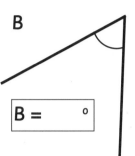

B = ____ °

C

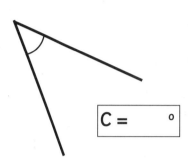

C = ____ °

D

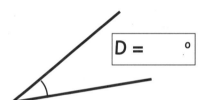

D = ____ °

E

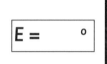

E = ____ °

F

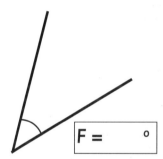

F = ____ °

G

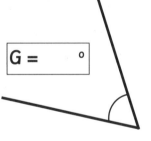

G = ____ °

H

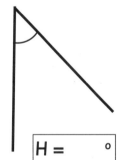

H = ____ °

I

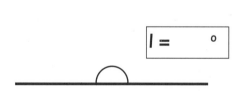

I = ____ °

✱ Answer these questions using the letter given to the angle.

1. Which is the largest angle? _____

2. Which is the smallest angle? _____

3. Which are right angles? _____

4. Which angle is 180°? _____

5. Which angles measure more than 40° but less than 60°? _____

6. Using the letters, write the angles in order from the largest to the smallest: _____

I can measure angles of 90°, 60°, 45° and 30° with set squares. ☐

Measures Market Game

Mental Starter

Learning Objective
- To identify patterns and relationships involving numbers, namely to count on and back in steps of 25 and then compare the pattern with steps of 250

Count on and back in 25s from 0 to 500.

What do we have to do to 25 to make it 250? Multiply it by 10.

Write 25, 50, 75, 100, 125 on the board.

Underneath 25 write 250 and underneath 50 write 500.

What comes next? 750, 1000, 1250 and so on.

What is the relationship involving these two patterns?

Establish that the first set of numbers have been multiplied by 10. Therefore they are the same numbers, but with a zero on the end.

Count on and back in 250s from 0 to 5000.

Learning Objectives

- To know the relationships between kilograms and grams, millilitres and litres
- To use their abbreviations

In addition:
- To use the fractions ½, ¼ and ¾ of quantities in measurements
- [icon] (Y4 and very able Y3) To use decimal notation to record measurements

Success Criteria

- I know the relationships between kilograms and grams, and litres and millilitres.
- I know the abbreviations for kilograms, grams, litres and millilitres.

CD-ROM Resources

- PowerPoint file
- Slide 7 in the PowerPoint file or an enlarged copy of the [icon] Activity Sheet to demonstrate
- Copies of the differentiated Activity Sheets

Other Resources

- Dice
- Coloured pencils (different colour for each player)

Introduction

Today we are going to play a game to practise converting measures to different formats; for example:
1200g = 1kg 200g and 1500ml = 1l 500ml or 1½ l

What do we measure mass (weight) in? Grams and kilograms.
What is the abbreviation for grams? g *kilograms?* kg
How many grams in one kilogram? 1000
What do we measure capacity (liquids) in? Millilitres and litres.
What is the abbreviation for millilitres? ml *litres?* l

What is ½ kilogram in grams? 500g
What is ¼ kilogram in grams? 250g
What is ¾ kilogram in grams? 750g

Write these on the board.

Repeat this for millilitres and litres, pointing out that the answers are the same.

What is 1500g in kg and grams? 1kg 500g

Give the children one minute to talk to the person sitting next to them about how they worked it out. Stress that you divide by 1000 when converting grams into kilograms and grams because there are 1000 grams in one kilogram. Give several more questions converting grams into kilograms and grams.

What about 2l 200ml in millilitres? 2200ml

Repeat the above activity using different quantities.

Y4 and very able Y3:
How can we write 3kg 400g in a shorter form, using just kg? 3.4kg
Explain that we don't need to write the whole 400g because the zeros are placeholders to show that there are no digits in those columns. When writing in decimal notation we just write the 4 as point 4. However, this only applies to zeros at the end of a number – 2kg 375g = 2.375kg.

Display the [icon] Activity Sheet to show the gameboard and demonstrate how to play the game.

Activity

AA [icon]
In pairs, these children should play the Measures Market Game, converting the decimal notation quantities they land on on the gameboard to the quantities on the shopping list; for example, 0.3kg = 300g. They can omit placeholders (zeros) at the end of a number, but must include other digits. If the quantity is the same, the player can tick their box on the shopping list for that item.

MA [icon]
In pairs, these children should play the game, converting the quantities they land on on the gameboard to the fractions of quantities on the shopping list; for example, 250g = ¼kg. If the quantity is the same, the player can tick their box for that item.

LA [icon] **& SEN**
In pairs or as a group (whichever is more appropriate), these children should play the game, converting the quantities they land on on the gameboard to the numbers and words on the shopping list; for example, 1000g of apples = 1 kilogram. If the quantity is the same, the player can tick their box for that item. **With support as appropriate.**

Key Vocabulary

kilograms, grams, millilitres, litres, abbreviations, measure, weight, capacity, mass, decimal notation, placeholders, convert

Plenary

What is ½ of 1000? 500
What is ¼ of 1000? 250
What is ¾ of 1000? 750
What is 1/10 of 1000? 100

What is 3600g in kg and g? 3kg 600g
What is it in decimal notation in kilograms? 3.6kg
What is 1½ l in litres and millilitres? 1l 500ml
What is it in decimal notation in litres? 1.5l

Repeat with similar conversions.

Year 4: *Can you explain why we don't use the zeros at the end of a quantity when we convert it to decimal notation?* Zeros are placeholders and so are not needed (unless there is a digit after a zero, as in 1.803kg).

Measures Market Game

Shopping List

1½l of apple juice		
1¾kg of apples		
¼kg of bread		
¾kg of cheese		
1¾kg of chicken		
¼l of cola		
½kg of grapes		
½l of milk		
¾kg of pork chops		
½l of shampoo		
¾kg of sugar		

Player 1 ☐ ☐ ☐ ☐ ☐ ☐ ☐ ☐ ☐ ☐ ☐

Player 2 ☐ ☐ ☐ ☐ ☐ ☐ ☐ ☐ ☐ ☐ ☐

Rules
- In pairs, take turns to throw the dice and move.
- When you land, check the item on your shopping list.
- Convert the quantity and if it is the same, tick your box next to the item.
- The winner is the one with the most items ticked off their list.

Game Board

HOME					
Shampoo 750ml	Bread 750g	Apple juice 250ml	Cola 1000ml	Grapes 250g	Cheese 1000g
Pork chop 1500g	Sugar 750g	Milk 1000ml	Apple (orange) 250ml	Chicken 1750g	Apple juice 1500ml
Chicken 1500g	Cola 250ml	Cheese 750g	Milk 2000ml	Apple juice 1000ml	Pork chop 250g
Sugar 1500g	Grapes 750g	Apple 750g	Pork chop 750g	Sugar 1000g	Shampoo 1250ml
START	Bread 500g	Shampoo 500ml	Chicken 2750g	Cola 2000ml	Apple 1750g
	Cheese 250g	Bread 250g	Chicken 1250g	Grapes 500g	Milk 500ml

I know the relationships between kg and g, and l and ml. ☐   I can use fractions of quantities. ☐

Mental Starter

Learning Objective
- To multiply and divide by 10 and 100

On their whiteboards, the children should show the answers to these questions after a count to ten:

What is?...

53 x 10
53 x 100
5300 ÷ 10
5300 ÷ 100
1.2 x 10
1.2 x 100
1200 ÷ 10
1200 ÷ 100

Ask questions randomly using x and ÷ by 10 and 100.

Learning Objectives

- To solve one-step problems involving money
- To add pairs of numbers using £ and p notation

Success Criteria
- I can add pairs of numbers using £ and p notation.

CD-ROM Resources
- PowerPoint file
- Copies of the Resource Sheet (preferably enlarged)
- Copies of the differentiated Activity Sheets

Other Resources

For the Mental Starter
- Whiteboards and pens

For the main activity
- Dice and counters
- Pencils
- Calculators (to check totals at end of game)

Introduction

Today we are going to play the Burger Bar Game, which involves adding.

How many pence in £1? 100p

How many pence in £10? 1000p

How did you work it out? 100p x 10

So, how many pence in £100? 10 000p

Remind the children that it is often easier to convert £ and p to pence, carry out the calculation and then divide by 100 to convert it back. For example, add £2.50 to £4.00:

250p + 400p = 650p.
650p = £6.50.

How much are the following in pence?
£3.95, £6.34, £19.99

How much are the following in £s and pence?
416p, 987p, 109p

What is a running total?
Demonstrate this. For example, on their first turn, Player 1 lands on an activity that costs £5.00, so £5.00 is written in the 'Cost of item' column and also in the 'Total spent' column. On the second and subsequent turns, the cost goes into the first column and is then added to the total spent column.

Player 1	
Cost of item	Total spent
£5.00	£5.00
£3.50	£8.50
£4.50	£13.00

Explain the activity.

Activity

The rules of the game are on the Resource Sheet with the gameboard.

The children should play in pairs, adding the cost of the item landed on as a running total on the tally sheet.

AA
For these children, the pence include a range of tens and units digits.

MA
For these children, the pence are in multiples of 5 and 10.

LA & SEN
These children should use money as an aid. Here the pence are also multiples of 5 and 10.
With support.

Key Vocabulary

£, pounds, p, pence, pennies, decimal point, decimals, amount, money, running total, convert, mentally, addition

Plenary

What is the highest running total?

What strategies did you use to carry out the calculations?

Did anyone use a different strategy?

Select children from each group to share their strategies with the class.

Burger Bar Game

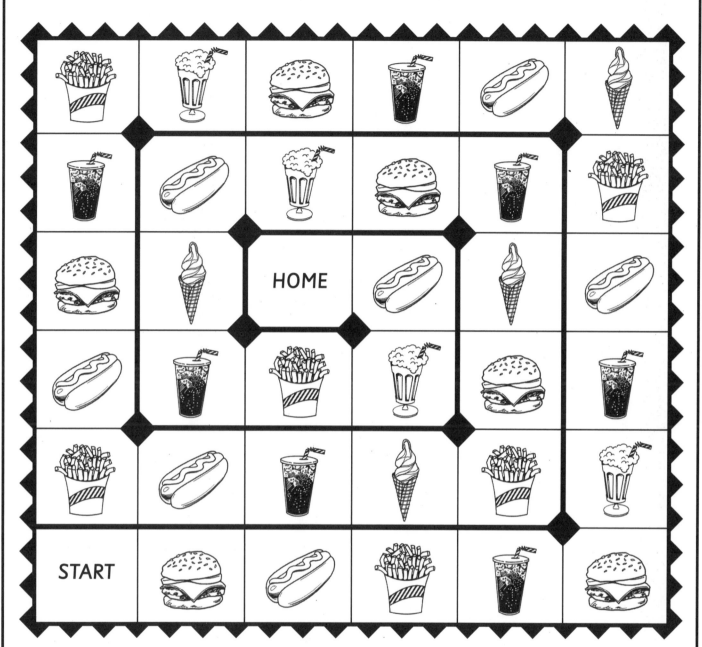

Rules

- Play with a partner, taking it in turns to go.
- Place your counters on START.
- Player 1 throws the dice, moves that number of spaces, uses Ben's Burger Bar Menu to find the cost of the item landed on, and writes the cost in both the 'Cost of item' and 'Total spent' columns.
- Player 2 then has their turn.
- After your first turns, write the cost of the item only in the 'Cost of item' column. Then add to the 'Total spent' amount for a running total.
- The players check each other's answers. They lose a turn if their calculation is incorrect.
- The winner is the first player to reach HOME.

Place Value Grids

Mental Starter	Learning Objectives	Introduction	Activity	Plenary
Learning Objective • To count on and back in multiples of 10, 100 and 1000 Begin counting back in 1s from 927 to 893, ensuring the children are secure in what happens when a 100 or 10s barrier is crossed. Count on in 10s from 34 to 154 and back. Repeat this using random starting and finishing numbers in multiples of 10, 100 and 1000.	• To use knowledge of place value up to 3 digits to complete a grid In addition: 📄 To use knowledge of place value up to 4 digits to complete a grid **Success Criteria** • I understand that every digit in a number has a value determined by its place in that number. **CD-ROM Resources** • PowerPoint file • Slide 5 in the PowerPoint file or an enlarged copy of Generic Sheet 7 (large 100 square) • Slide 7 in the PowerPoint file or an enlarged copy of the 📄 Activity Sheet • Copies of the differentiated Activity Sheets • Copies of Generic Sheet 6 or 7 (small and large 100 squares) • Answers Sheet **Other Resources** • Pencils	*Today we are going to complete some place value grids.* *What does 'place value' mean?* Every digit in a number has a value determined by its place in that number. Demonstrate t h t u. Write 3942 on the board. *What is the value of the 9?* 900 Repeat this for each digit. Repeat the process for other numbers. Now display a 100 square (Generic Sheet 7). *Who can show me the answer to 33+1 on this 100 square?* Repeat the question, using +10, −1 and −10. *Using your knowledge of place value, which digit changes when we add 10; 100; 1000?* Repeat this for subtraction. Display the 📄 Activity Sheet. Explain that this is the activity that they will be completing, although some of them will be working with different numbers. As a whole class, complete one or two lines. Emphasise that care is essential. *If I add 10, what will be the answer?*	The children should be reminded to work on one horizontal row first, referring back to the central number or other given numbers each time, before completing each calculation. **AA** 📄 These children should complete the grid that has numbers with up to 4 digits. **MA** 📄 These children should complete the grid that has numbers with up to 3 digits. **LA** 📄 These children should complete the grid that has numbers with up to 3 digits. They can use a 100 square and/or number line for support. **Teacher support if required.** **SEN** These children should do the same as the LA children but with support.	Work through the 📄 Activity Sheet with the whole class. Write on the board 48 301. *What is the value of the 4?* Repeat this with other numbers. Ask the children what would be the value of the digit if you were increasing it by 10 000 each time. For example, what would the value of the 4 be if we increased the number by 10 000? *Who knows the value of the first digit after a decimal point?* 1/10th.

Key Vocabulary

place value, digit, number, hundreds, tens, units, count on/back, add, subtract, placeholder, horizontal

Place Value Grid

✱ Complete this table. Remember to check the given numbers to see if you are right.

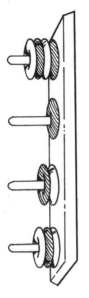

+100	+10	+1	Numbers	−1	−10	−100
			725			625
			329		319	
	244		234			
			160		880	
			508			
			634	406		
			116			

I understand place value up to 3 digits. ☐

Partitioning Game

Mental Starter

Learning Objective
- To practise halving and doubling

Play 'Halves Bingo'.

Ask the children to draw a 3 x 2 grid on their whiteboards. They should write any odd number between 11 and 29 in each box.

Call out even numbers randomly between 22 and 58.

If they have a number that is half the number that has been called out, the children should put a cross through it.

As you go along, write the number called and its half on the board so the children can check as they go.

The first child with all their numbers crossed out calls 'Bingo!'

Repeat this, increasing the value of the numbers.

Learning Objectives

- To partition 3- and 4-digit numbers

In addition:
- 🎲 To partition 4- and 5-digit numbers

Success Criteria

- I can partition 3- and 4-digit numbers.

CD-ROM Resources

- PowerPoint file
- Copies of the differentiated Resource Sheets
- Copies of the Activity Sheet (Score Sheet)
- Generic Sheet 6 or 7 (small and large 100 squares) for SEN children, if required

Other Resources

For the Mental Starter
- Whiteboards and pens

For the main activity
- Dice
- Counters
- Pencils

For SEN children
- Whiteboards and pens

Introduction

Today we are going to partition numbers.

What does 'place value' mean?
Every digit in a number has a value determined by its place in that number.

Write 192 on the board.

What is the value of the 9 in this number? 90

Demonstrate th h t u. Write 3942 on the board.

What is the value of the 9 in this number? 900.

Partition 3942 into 1000, 100, 10 and 1s.

What is the value of each digit? 3000, 900, 40, 2

Repeat the process for other numbers.

In the number 3105 what job does the 0 do? What is it called? It shows that this place is for a digit that has a value, which in this case is 0 (zero). It means there are no 10s in this number. It is called a placeholder.

Demonstrate how we use zeros as placeholders. Write 4328 on the board and then 4000 + ☐ + 20 + 8.

What is the missing number? What is its value?

Repeat this with other number sentences.

What value does the 1 have in 14 235?

Write various 3-, 4- and 5-digit numbers on the board.

What is the value of this digit?

What is this number in words?

Explain the activity and how to use the score sheets (Activity Sheet). Explain that partitioned sentences must be set out as in the example below.

| 3412 | 3000 + 400 + 10 + 2 |

Activity

The rules of the game are on the Resource Sheets with the gameboards. The children should play in pairs.

AA 🎲🎲

These children should play the game, writing out and then partitioning whichever 4- or 5-digit number they land on.

Extension: How many different numbers can be made from these digits: 6, 4, 5, 3 and 1? Put them in order of size.

MA 🎲🎲

These children should play the game, writing out and then partitioning whichever 3- or 4-digit number they land on.

Extension: How many different numbers can be made from these digits: 6, 4, 5 and 1? Put them in order of size.

LA 🎲

These children should play the game, writing out and then partitioning whichever 2- or 3-digit number they land on.

Extension: How many different numbers can be made from these digits: 6, 4 and 1? Put them in order of size. **Support as appropriate.**

SEN

These children should use a dice to generate some digits, and then write the digits on their whiteboards in the order that makes the highest number they can. They should then compare their answers. **With support.**

Key Vocabulary

halving, doubling, place value, digit, number, thousands, hundreds, tens, units, count on/back, add, subtract, placeholder, greatest value, least value, between, ten thousand

Plenary

Write the following number on the board:

48 301

What is the value of the 4?

And the 8?

Repeat this with other numbers.

What is the largest number you can make using the digits 1, 7, 4 and 2?

What is the smallest?

Can you use those digits to make a number between 3200 and 4200?

4127 or 4172

What is the value of the digit after a decimal point?
1/10th

Partitioning Game

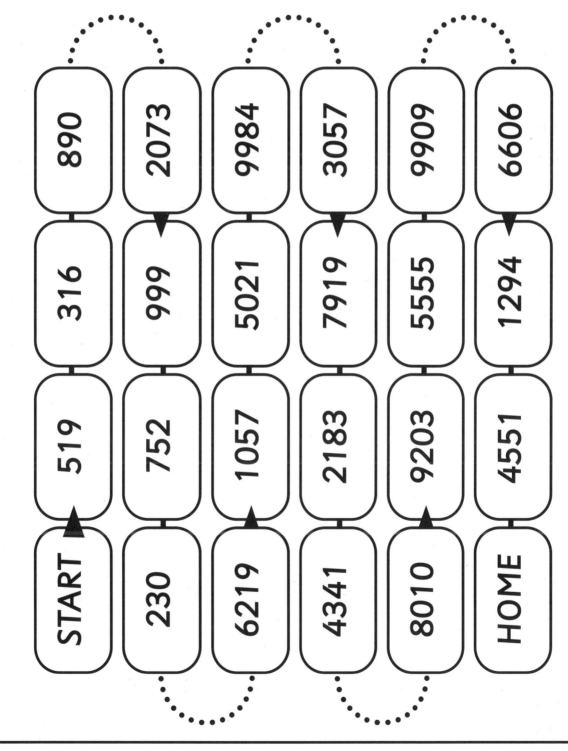

Rules

- Play in pairs, taking it in turns to throw the dice and move.

- When a player lands on a number, you both write it in the first column on your own Score Sheet.

- Then you both partition the number – e.g. 3412 = 3000 + 400 + 10 + 2

- Compare your partitioned sentences.

- If you both agree, the player who landed on the number scores a point by placing a 1 in the third column. Then it is the other player's turn.

- If you disagree, discuss your strategies, write the partitioned sentences again and compare. However, if your original answer was correct, you still only score one point!

- The winner is the player with the most points for correct answers.

Remember! You can only score a point on your turn.

Game board numbers:

START	519	316	890
230	752	999	2073
6219	1057	5021	9984
4341	21183	7919	3057
8010	9203	5555	9909
HOME	4551	1294	6606

Compass Points Shapes

Mental Starter

Learning Objective
- To know the 4 points of the compass

Play the compass game.

- Designate areas in the classroom for each of the 4 compass points and stick a label up at each point.
- When you call out the name of a point the children must turn to face it.
- The slowest child(ren) is (are) eliminated.

You might like to tell the children that the Arctic is in the North and the Antarctic in the South. On the Resource Sheet is a compass and four animals – the ones at the top are two of many that can be found in the Arctic region and the ones at the bottom are two of many to be found in the Antarctic region.

Learning Objectives

- To use the 8-point compass to describe directions
- To write instructions to draw a shape using the 8 points of a compass

Success Criteria

- I can use compass points to direct someone to make a set shape by walking.

CD-ROM Resources

- PowerPoint file
- Slide 4 in the PowerPoint file or an enlarged copy of the Resource Sheet with the letters of the points removed
- Slide 5 in the PowerPoint file or an enlarged copy of the Activity Sheet
- Copies of the Resource Sheet
- Copies of the Activity Sheet
- Answers Sheet

Other Resources

- Squared paper
- Pencils
- Sticky tack

Introduction

Today we are going to write directions to make shapes, using the 8 points of a compass.

Draw an 8-point compass on the board or display the Resource Sheet.

What are the 8 points of a compass?
N, S, E, W, NE, NW, SE, SW

Can you label this compass correctly?

Select some children to come up and label it. (Ask LA children to only label the four main points.)

Demonstrate writing instructions for drawing a square on the Activity Sheet. Remind the children that North remains static, so each move needs to relate to the position of North.

Start facing North.
a) Face E and move 4 steps.
b) Face S and move 4 steps.
c) Face W and move 4 steps.
d) Face N and move 4 steps.

Explain that one line of instructions is required for each side of a shape.

Can you write directions like this for a triangle?

Ask for volunteers to come up and have a go. (See the Answers Sheet for one version of a triangle.)

Explain the activity.

Activity

North must be the starting point to determine the destination compass point each time the children begin to draw a side, otherwise it would be very difficult to make a shape using the 8 compass points. They should refer to the compass on their Record Sheet (Activity Sheet) before writing each instruction.

AA
In pairs, these children should agree, but record individually, directions to draw a kite (diamond) using the compass points.
Extension: They could repeat this for a rhombus. Then they could investigate whether a regular pentagon could be drawn using this method.

MA
In pairs, these children should agree, but record individually, directions to draw a rectangle using compass points.
Extension: They could repeat this for a kite (diamond).

LA & SEN
In a group, these children should agree, but record individually, directions to draw a square using the compass points.
With support.
Extension: They could repeat this for a rectangle.

Key Vocabulary

horizontal, vertical, diagonal, N, S, W, E, NW, NE, SE, SW, directions, vertex, vertices, sides, shape, compass points, square, triangle, rectangle, kite, rhombus

Plenary

Select two children to test another group's directions – one to read them, one to follow them at the front of the classroom.

Are the directions clear?

Did the directions instruct you to form the correct shape?

Play the compass game (from the Mental Starter), but using the 8 compass points instead of 4.

Compass Points Shapes

What's My Name?

Mental Starter

Learning Objective
- To describe 2-D shapes by their properties

The children sit in a circle. Only the child with the feely bag can speak.

Ask the children to pass the feely bag round the circle. Select a child to place their hand in the bag and choose one shape without taking their hand out of the bag and without looking at it.

Ask the child to describe the properties of the shape by feel and try to guess the name of the shape.

The rest of the class can guess too as the child describes it.

The child should then remove the shape from the bag and show it to the class.

Were they right?

What other properties could they have described?

Continue passing the feely bag round and repeat the process.

Learning Objective
- To sort 2-D shapes by their properties

Success Criteria
- I can sort 2-D shapes by their properties.

CD-ROM Resources
- PowerPoint file
- Slides 5–10 in the PowerPoint file or an enlarged version of the Resource Sheet
- Slide 11 in the PowerPoint file or an enlarged version of the Activity Sheet
- Copies of the differentiated Activity Sheets
- Answers Sheet

Other Resources

For the Mental Starter
- A feely bag – can be an envelope or box, but nothing transparent
- A selection of 2-D shapes

Introduction

Today we are going to guess some shapes by their properties and then sort them.

What is a 2-D shape? A flat shape, which has length and breadth (as opposed to a 3-D shape, such as a cube, which has length, breadth and height).

What is a polygon?
Any 2-D shape with three or more sides and angles.

What is a regular polygon?
All the sides and angles are the same.

What is an irregular polygon?
All the sides and angles are not the same.

What words can we use to help us describe the properties of 2-D shapes?
Sides (edges), vertex, vertices (corners), right angles, angles, equal, lines of symmetry, parallel, opposite sides and so on.

Show some shapes on the board, using the Resource Sheet, but covering the descriptions. Point to a shape.

What is the name of this shape?

Can you describe the properties of this shape?

Work through the shapes, revealing the descriptions as you go.

Now we are going to sort these shapes using an identification key.

Display Activity Sheet on the board and use it with the whole class to demonstrate how identification keys work. Leave it on the board for the AA children to refer to during their task, as they will be creating their own keys.

Explain the activity.

Activity

AA
In pairs, these children should design their own identification key to sort the properties of six shapes of their choice, using the displayed Activity Sheet to refer to if required. **Initial guidance from a teacher will be required.**

MA
These children should sort the seven 2-D shapes on their sheet by their properties.
Extension: In pairs, on blank paper, they could make up a 2-D shapes quiz, using their properties as questions. For example, What's My Name? I have 3 sides, 3 angles and the angles all add up to 180°.

LA & SEN
These children should take it in turns to use the feely bag, describing the properties of a shape while the others try to guess which shape it is.
With support.
Extension: They could sort a range of shapes using the Identification Key on Activity Sheet .

Key Vocabulary

2-D shapes, 3-D shapes, polygon, regular, irregular, quadrilateral, square, triangle, rectangle, circle, pentagon, rhombus, hexagon, octagon, properties, sides, vertex, vertices, corners, right angles, parallel lines

Plenary

Try out one of the identification keys that the group made.

Did it enable us to sort the shapes effectively?

Were the facts correct?

What other properties could they have used for these shapes?

Can you think of any other criteria we could have used to sort these shapes?

Additional activity: as a whole class, teacher-led, play the quiz game that the group devised.

What's My Name? Identification Key

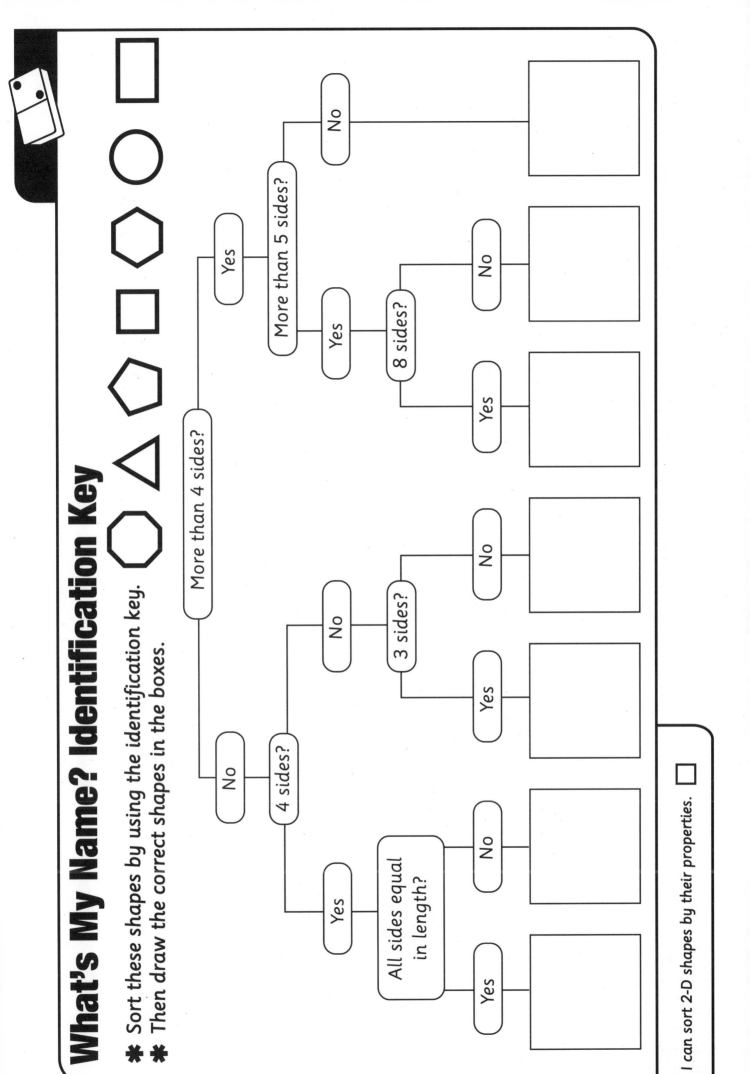

✱ Sort these shapes by using the identification key.

✱✱ Then draw the correct shapes in the boxes.

More than 4 sides?

Yes → More than 5 sides?
- No
- Yes → 8 sides?
  - No
  - Yes

No → 4 sides?
- No → 3 sides?
  - No
  - Yes
- Yes → All sides equal in length?
  - No
  - Yes

I can sort 2-D shapes by their properties. ☐

Mental Starter	Learning Objective	Introduction	Activity	Plenary

Mental Starter

Learning Objective
- To revise reading hourly and half-hourly time

Using an open-faced clock, setting times first for hours, ask these questions.

What's the time?

What does the little hand show?

Big hand?

How many minutes are there in an hour? In half an hour?

What happens to the hour hand when the clock says half past?
It moves to half-way between the last hour and the next one.

Set some times at half past.

What time is it?

How many minutes past is that?

Remind and show children that one half of the clock is past the hour, the other half is to the hour.

Learning Objective
- To read 12-hour analogue and digital clocks to the nearest 5 minutes

Success Criteria
- I can read 12-hour analogue and digital clocks to the nearest 5 minutes.

CD-ROM Resources
- PowerPoint file
- Copies of the differentiated Activity Sheets

Other Resources
- Clocks for demonstration

Introduction

Today we are going to read the time on a 12-hour clock, to the nearest minute or 5 minutes.

Set the analogue clock to quarter past ten.

What time is it?

How many minutes past the hour is this? 15

Explain that the numbers round the clock are placed at exactly five-minute intervals. Point out that each five-minute section is partitioned into 5 x 1 minutes and also that each five-minute section represents one hour for the hour hand.

Move the clock to a quarter to 5.

What time is it?

Reinforce that this means there is a quarter of an hour to go to the next hour.

How many minutes past 4 is this? 45

Remind the children to use their 5x tables: 9 x 5 = 45.

Explain that on an analogue clock we would read it as a quarter to 5, but on a digital clock it would show only minutes past the hour, in this case 4:45.

Explain that we often say 20 to 5 (using the 'to' side) rather than 4:40.

Tell the children that they are going to be clocks and their arms are the hands. Leave the analogue clock on show for them to refer to. Ask them to stand. Call out a time. They should move their arms to where the hour and minute hands should be. 4:30, 7:15, quarter to 9, 20 past 6, 10 to 1 and so on.

Explain the activity.

Activity

AA
These children should complete the schedule by writing the time stated in the activity onto the clocks, indicating am and pm on the digital version. They should write and show the time they go to bed.
Extension: Ask them to use the back of the sheet to write what they do on a weekend day, with the times.

MA
These children should complete the schedule by writing the time stated in the activity onto the clocks. The times are in multiples of 5 minutes. They should write and show the time they go to bed.
Extension: They should use the back of their sheets to make up some of their own times.

LA
These children should complete the schedule by writing the time stated in the activity onto the clocks. Only o'clock and half past times are used. They should write and show the time they go to bed.
Extension: What other things do they do at school? Ask them to turn the page over, draw some clocks with times on them and write what it is they do.

SEN
These children should write the time on the analogue and digital clocks.
With support.
Extension: They could try the Activity Sheet.

Key Vocabulary

time, clock, analogue, digital, schedule, o'clock, half past, quarter to, half past, past, to, hours, minutes, seconds, minute hand, hour hand, second hand

---

Plenary

The children in the AA group could show the class what they do at the weekend, demonstrating the times by using the open-faced clock.

Children from all groups can demonstrate on the clock things they do at different times of the day.

Time for School

✳ Fill in the correct time on these clocks.

	☐ ☐ : ☐ ☐	I get up at half past seven. Then I have my breakfast.
	☐ ☐ : ☐ ☐	I get dressed, get my bag ready and leave for school at twenty minutes to nine.
	☐ ☐ : ☐ ☐	The school bell goes at ten to nine and I go into the classroom.
	☐ ☐ : ☐ ☐	We stop for lunch at five past twelve.
	☐ ☐ : ☐ ☐	I leave the school at a quarter past three.
	☐ ☐ : ☐ ☐	I eat my tea at ten minutes past five.
	☐ ☐ : ☐ ☐	I go to bed at _____

I can read 12-hour analogue and digital clocks to the nearest 5 minutes. ☐

What's My Word?

Learning Objective

- To practise dictionary skills

Success Criteria

- I can find new or unusual words in the dictionary.

CD-ROM Resources

- PowerPoint file
- Slide 4 in the PowerPoint file or an enlarged copy of the Resource Sheet
- Copies of the Activity Sheet, cut up

Other Resources

- Dictionaries
- Pens

Introduction

Today we are going to revise how to use a dictionary and then play a game called 'What's My Word?'

How are words listed in a dictionary? Alphabetically.

What other uses does a dictionary have apart from checking the spelling of a word? It gives a definition of the word.

Did you know that often the dictionary will tell you what word class a word is?

What is a word class? For example, a noun, adjective, verb or adverb.

Sometimes a dictionary will tell you how to pronounce a word.

Display the sample page from a dictionary (Resource Sheet). Ask the children to look for the word 'school'.

What do we look for first?
- *First we find a word beginning with s.*
- *Next we look for a word that has the next letter in the word – c.*
- *Now we look for a word that has the third letter in the word – h.*

We continue to look for a word with the next letter in the word until we have found the correct word.

In pairs, look up the word 'grate' in your own dictionary.

NB: Dictionaries may differ across ability groups.

What page number is it on?

Repeat this for the word 'tease'.

Show the children the word slips on the Activity Sheet and explain the activity. Model a word for them on the board.

Activity

PAIRS, WITHIN SAME ABILITY GROUPS

Give each pair a dictionary appropriate to its ability.

Differentiation is, therefore, in the complexity of the new words chosen and the dictionary each group uses.

Individually, the children should find a new or unusual word they like in the dictionary. They should then fill out a 'What's My Word?' slip (Activity Sheet) with the details.

Each child should find their partner's word in their dictionary and check that the details on the slip are correct. They should put a tick (if correct) or cross (if incorrect) and write their initials in the small box at the bottom of the slip.

They should then write the word and the page number from the dictionary on the back of the slip (as proof that it has been looked up) and return the slip to their partner. They continue playing until the teacher asks them to stop.

If appropriate, partners can swap so that different pairs play together each time.

Support as required.

Key Vocabulary

dictionary, alphabetical, alphabetically, spelling, word class, noun, adjective, verb, adverb, pronounce, pronunciation, letter

Plenary

Select children from different ability groups to challenge the class with their words.

What new or interesting words have you found?

Was it a new word or an unusual one?

Did any words have more than one meaning? How did you record that?

What's My Word?

What's My Word?

It begins with ....
It has .... letters.
It has .... vowels.
It means: ....
....
....

What's My Word?

It begins with ....
It has .... letters.
It has .... vowels.
It means: ....
....
....

What's My Word?

It begins with ....
It has .... letters.
It has .... vowels.
It means: ....
....
....

What's My Word?

It begins with ....
It has .... letters.
It has .... vowels.
It means: ....
....
....

What's My Word?

It begins with ....
It has .... letters.
It has .... vowels.
It means: ....
....
....

Cool Collective Nouns

Learning Objectives	Introduction	Activity	Plenary
• To understand the term 'collective noun' and collect examples • To invent collective nouns	**Today we are going to look at some common collective nouns and then make up our own.** **What is a noun?** A person, place or thing, such as a table or a box. **What examples of nouns can you give me?** **What is a collective noun?** A term given to a word that describes a group of things or people. Display the Resource Sheet and ask for volunteers to come up and match a collective noun from the ones in the box with one of the pictures.	Differentiation is primarily through the choice of new words, the level of dictionary and by outcome. **AA** Individually, these children should think of collective nouns for the example nouns on the Activity Sheet, then select their own nouns and invent as many new, good collective nouns as they can, remembering to describe the noun's characteristics, actions or looks. Tell them that they can make up new collective nouns for ones that already exist, if they feel their choice is more appropriate. They may use a dictionary to find new nouns. **Extension:** They could write a sentence for each of their favourite collective nouns.	Share some of the children's invented collective nouns, ensuring that all ability groups have an opportunity to read theirs to the class. **Does the collective noun describe the characteristics, actions or appearance of the noun?**
Success Criteria			
• I understand what a collective noun is. • I can invent some collective nouns of my own.	**What other collective nouns can you think of that we use in everyday speech or writing?** A crew of sailors, a clutch of eggs, a litter of kittens, a gaggle of geese, a pod of whales, a forest of trees. Find some more difficult ones to introduce to the children, such as a bench of judges and a hand of bananas. Why do the children think 'bench' and 'hand' are appropriate?	**MA** These children should do the same activity but work in pairs. **Extension:** They could illustrate and label each of their favourite collective nouns. **LA & SEN** In pairs, or in a group, whichever is appropriate, these children should complete the same activity. **With support and scribed for the children if required.**	
CD-ROM Resources			
• PowerPoint file • Slide 3 in the PowerPoint file or an enlarged copy of the Resource Sheet • Copies of the Activity Sheet	Tell the children that they are going to make up some of their own collective nouns, matching the characteristics, actions or appearance of the noun used; for example, a bossy of teachers, a chattering of children, a spectacle of opticians, a giggle of comedians and a calculator of accountants.	**Key Vocabulary**	
Other Resources		**noun, term, collective noun, characteristics, actions, appearance**	
• Dictionaries • Pens	To help the children with their task, mind-map some nouns and write them on the board. Include people, animals and objects. Talk the children through the Activity Sheet. Explain that some nouns are already there for them to think of collective nouns for, and then they have to think of collective nouns for other things, such as those just mind-mapped.		

Cool Collective Nouns

of flowers

of musicians

of cards

of sheep

of fish

of soldiers

of bees

of footballers

of elephants

of ants

of lions

of people

Collective Nouns

band	team	flock	army	group	herd
bouquet	school	colony	pack	pride	swarm

Adverb Blockbuster Game

Learning Objective	Introduction	Activity	Plenary
• To know that an adverb describes a verb and adds depth of description	**Today we are going to revise adverbs and play an adverb game.**	**IN ABILITY GROUPS**	Select children from each group to read out some of their adverbs.
Success Criteria	**What is an adverb?** An adverb enhances a verb, describing how the action of the verb is carried out.	All the children should play the Blockbuster Adverb Game in two teams per table.	**Is it an adverb?**
• I can use adverbs to describe how a verb is performed.	Write the words 'verb' and 'adverb' on the board.	Make sure they have understood the rules (Resource Sheet 2). Read through them together, stopping to explain where necessary.	**What could it describe?** Ask them to read their sentences.
	Next, write the word 'eat' on the board. Ask a child to come out to the front of the class and demonstrate eating. Agree that 'eat' is a verb.	Although the rules state that the children should have two minutes to find a word, you should amend this according to your class.	**Does the adverb describe the verb well?**
CD-ROM Resources	**How does s/he eat?** Ask the children to suggest some adverbs for this; for example, 'greedily'. The child demonstrating should then act out the verb and adverb, in this instance by eating greedily.	**AA & MA** ⚂ These children should use adverbs in their sentences.	Remind the children that adverbs are not always after the verb in a sentence. Varying its position in the sentence adds variety to their writing. For example, using the adverb 'continuously':
• PowerPoint file • Slide 6 in the PowerPoint file or an enlarged copy of Resource Sheet 1 • Copies of Resource Sheets 1 and 2	Repeat this with other adverbs for 'eat'. Repeat with other verbs and adverbs.	**LA** ⚀ **& SEN** These children should play in two teams, supported and scribed for as required.	*The dog was barking <u>continuously</u>.*
	What do you notice about the ending of most adverbs? They end in 'ly'.		*The dog, who was <u>continuously</u> barking, was hungry.*
	Elicit examples of adverbs from the children and write them on the board.		*The <u>continuously</u> barking dog was hungry.*
Other Resources	**What steps do we need to take to look words up in a dictionary?** Briefly discuss the method with the children.		*<u>Continuously</u>, the dog barked, disturbing the peaceful Sunday afternoon.*
• Coloured counters – 10 counters of the same colour per team • Lined paper • Pens • Dictionaries • Coin or dice per table	**What is a word class?** It tells us what sort of word a word is, such as a noun or verb. Model how to look up the word class of the word. Explain the abbreviations (such as n for noun) to the children and write them on the board. Tell them to use these clues to help them.	**Key Vocabulary**	
	Display the gameboard (Resource Sheet 1) and explain and demonstrate the game. Tell the children that while they are waiting for the playing team to choose a word, they can plan their strategy for their next move.	**adverb, verb, word class, description, enhance, dictionary, abbreviation**	

Adverb Blockbuster Game

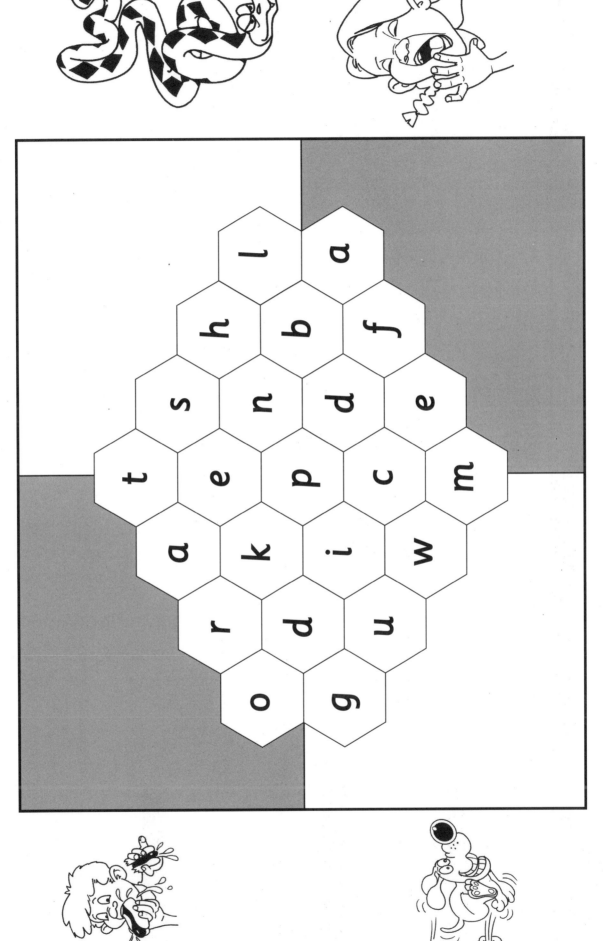

Cutting Compound Words

Learning Objective

- To understand that a compound word is two smaller words joined together

Success Criteria

- I understand that a compound word is two smaller words joined together.

CD-ROM Resources

- PowerPoint file
- Slide 3 in the PowerPoint file or an enlarged copy of the Resource Sheet
- Copies of the differentiated Activity Sheets

Other Resources

- Lined paper for the group
- Pens
- Dictionaries
- Reading books

Introduction

Today we are going to look at compound words.

What is a compound word?
A word made up of two other words, such as class + room = classroom.

Display the Resource Sheet and read it through as a class.

What compound words can you find in the text?

Select children to identify and underline a compound word. They should then tell the class which two smaller words it is made up from.

Repeat this until all the compound words have been identified: (weekend, homework, handkerchief, grandmother, armchair, tiptoed, sideboard, cupboard, something, upstairs, bedroom, handrail, handbag, downstairs, beside, tablecloth, textbook, worksheet)

What other compound words can you think of?

Write the children's suggestions on the board. Give them some examples of your own, such as dustbin, paintbrush, playground, clockwise, blackboard and whiteboard.

Explain to the children that most, but not all, compound words are nouns.

What is a noun? A person, place or thing.

Explain the activity.

Activity

AA
These children should think of a topic or short story. They should write it out on lined paper, using as many compound words as possible, while retaining the sense. Compound words may be taken from the example text, the list on the board, a dictionary and their reading books.

Extension: Using a dictionary, they should find some new compound words and list them beneath their writing, separating them into their two smaller words.

MA
These children should identify the compound words illustrated on their sheet and separate them into their two smaller words. They should then write the compound words and smaller words in the spaces.

Extension: Using a dictionary or their reading book, they should find new compound words and list them on the back of their sheet, separating them into their two smaller words.

LA
These children should read the compound words on their sheet, with the help of the illustrations, then separate them into their two smaller words and write them in the spaces.

Extension: Using a dictionary or their reading book, they should find new compound words and list them on the sheet, separating them into their two smaller words as in the task.

SEN
These children should read the compound word, then write the two separate words in the spaces on their sheets, using the picture clues.
Support as appropriate.

Key Vocabulary

compound word, noun, separate

Plenary

Share some of the paragraphs that the group have written.

Ask the other groups:
What compound word did you identify?

What two smaller words were joined together to form it?

Repeat.

Who can give me a new compound word that we haven't used yet?

Cutting Compound Words

✱ Write the compound word. Then write the two separate words that make up the compound word. Use a dictionary to help you with the spelling.

  _____ = _____ + _____

  _____ = _____ + _____

  _____ = ____ + _____

  _____ = _____ + ____

  _____ = _____ + _____

  _____ = _____ + _____

  _____ = ____ + ____

  _____ = ___ + ____

  _____ = ___ + _____

  _____ = ____ + ____

I can identify the two words that join together to make a compound word. ☐

Granny's Gruesome Grammar Goulash

Learning Objectives

- To revise word classes
- To use word classes to write a recipe poem

Success Criteria

- I can use word classes to write a recipe poem.

CD-ROM Resources

- PowerPoint file
- Copies of the Resource Sheet – one copy between two children
- Copies of the Activity Sheet

Other Resources

- Lined paper
- Pens

Introduction

Today we are going to write a recipe with gruesome ingredients, using all the word classes.

What is a word class?
E.g. a verb, adverb, noun, adjective.

What is a noun? Can you give me an example?
What is an adjective? Can you give me an example?
What is a verb? Can you give me an example?
What is an adverb? Can you give me an example?

Explain to the children that they are going to write a list poem – a recipe for Granny's gruesome grammar goulash, using really horrible ingredients. Model using verbs, adverbs, nouns and adjectives in a recipe poem:

Place all these ingredients in a pot:
Pull two hairs from the head of a grumbling old man,
Peel a wart from a smelly boy's finger,
Bring to the boil, then simmer for 4 hours,
Serve with crusty bread.

As a whole class, identify and underline the individual word classes using a different colour for each.

Brainstorm some awful adjectives and some vile verbs.

How can we add adverbs to the lines?
'Roughly pull', 'Thinly peel', 'Serve carefully' and so on.

Remind the children to begin each line with a capital letter and end each with a comma. The last word of the poem must have a full stop at the end. Each line must include at least one nasty noun and one awful adjective.

Explain the activity and give out copies of the Resource Sheet, if required.

Activity

Differentiation is by outcome.

AA
On the Activity Sheet, these children should make up a recipe poem at least eight lines long, using gruesome ingredients. They should include a verb and at least one noun, adjective and adverb in each line.

MA
On the Activity Sheet, these children should also make up a recipe poem of at least six lines that includes a verb and at least one noun and adjective in each line.

LA & SEN
These children should make up a recipe poem using gruesome ingredients on the Activity Sheet. They must use at least one noun and adjective in each line.
Support or scribe if appropriate.

Key Vocabulary

noun, adjective, verb, adverb, word class, grammar, punctuation, capital letters, full stops, commas, vocabulary

Plenary

Select children from all ability groups to share their recipe poems.

Were the ingredients gruesome?

Could you hear a noun?

Could you hear a verb?

Could you hear an adjective?

Could you hear an adverb?

Granny's Gruesome Grammar Goulash

Place all these ingredients in a pot:

_____

_____

_____

_____

_____

_____

_____

Bring to the boil, then simmer for 4 hours,

Serve with crusty bread.

I can use nouns and adjectives to write a poem. ☐

Prefix Perfection Game

Learning Objective	Introduction	Activity	Plenary
• To recognise a range of prefixes and understand how they modify meaning and spelling	**Today we are going to look at the prefixes 'dis', 'mis' and 'un', and then play a game matching the prefixes to the root words.** **What is a prefix?** Letters that are added to the beginning of a word to change its meaning, such as 'un' – fair/unfair, kind/unkind.	**AA** In pairs, these children should decide whether any or all of the prefixes 'dis', 'mis' and 'un' can be added to the root word landed on, to make a new word. They should then write the root word and the new word(s), with the prefix(es) added, on their lined paper.	**What does the prefix 'dis' mean?** 'Not' or 'the opposite of'. **So what does the word 'dislike' mean?** Not like. Disagree? Dishonest?
Success Criteria	**What is a root word?** A word that can have a prefix or suffix added to it, such as 'fair' – unfair, fairly, fairness. (You may decide to explain what a suffix is very briefly at this stage.)	**MA** In pairs, these children should decide whether either or both of the prefixes 'dis' and 'un' can be added to the root word landed on, to make a new word. They should write the root word and the new word(s), with the prefix(es) added, on their lined paper.	**What does 'mis' mean?** 'Wrong' or 'false'. **So what does the word 'miscount' mean?** Count wrongly.
• I can match the root word with the correct prefix or prefixes.	**What does 'dis' mean?** 'Not' or 'the opposite of'. **What words can you think of that begin with the prefix 'dis', remembering that the prefix must change the meaning of the root word?** Examples are: disused, discount, discover, dislike, disease, distrust, dishonest and displease.		Misread? Misfit?
CD-ROM Resources	**What does 'mis' mean?** 'Wrong' or 'false'.	**LA & SEN** In pairs or a group, whichever is appropriate, these children should play the game, determining whether the prefix 'un' can be added to the root word landed on, to make a new word. They should write the root word and the new word, with the prefix added, on their lined paper. Some of the words are not able to take the prefix. **Support where appropriate.**	**What does 'un' mean?** 'Not'. **So what does the word 'unlucky' mean?** Not lucky.
• The PowerPoint file • Slide 5 in the PowerPoint file or an enlarged version of the Resource Sheet • Copies of the differentiated Resource Sheets (the gameboards) • Answers Sheet	**What words can you think of that begin with the prefix 'mis', remembering that the prefix must change the meaning of the root word?** Examples are: misused, miscount, mistrust, misread, misbelieve, misfit, misplace and mistake. **What does 'un' mean?** 'Not'		Uncover? Unfair?
Other Resources	**What words can you think of that begin with the prefix 'un', remembering that the prefix must change the meaning of the root word?** Examples are: unused, uncover, unlike, unable, unease, unconnected, unfit, unbelief and unusual.	**Key Vocabulary**	
Per pair of children: • Dice • Two different coloured counters • A dictionary • Lined paper • Pens	**What do you notice about the spelling of the new word?** The spelling of the root word doesn't change when the prefix is added. Using the enlarged version of the Resource Sheet, explain the game. Point out that the rules are on the gameboards. Read through the displayed set together.	prefix, prefixes, root word	

Prefix Perfection Gameboard

Rules

- Play with a partner, taking it in turns to go.
- Place your counters on START.
- Player 1 throws the dice and moves that number of spaces.
- Decide if the word landed on can take the prefix 'dis' or 'un' or both.
- Write the root word on your sheet of paper. Then rewrite it, complete with the prefix or prefixes below it.
- If you are unsure, check the words in the dictionary.
- If the word you landed on can take both prefixes, score 2 points. If it can only take one prefix, score 1 point.
- The second player takes their turn.
- Keep a tally of your score on the back of your sheet of paper.
- The winner is the player who has scored the most points.

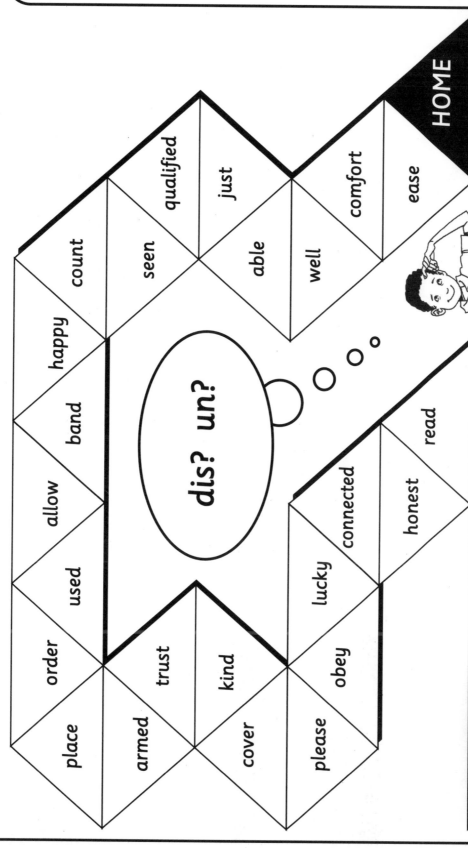

dis? un?

HOME

qualified
just
comfort
ease

count
seen
able
well

happy
band

allow

used

order
armed

trust
kind
cover

lucky
connected
honest
read
fair

obey
please

stable
like
agree

START

Learning Objectives

- To create roles showing how behaviour can be interpreted from different viewpoints
- To identify and discuss qualities of others' performances, including gesture and action

Success Criteria

- I can create roles showing how behaviour can be interpreted from different viewpoints.

CD-ROM Resources

- PowerPoint file
- Slide 3 in the PowerPoint file or copies of Resource Sheet 1 for the children to share
- Slide 5 in the PowerPoint file
- Copies of Resource Sheet 2

Other Resources

- Paper to jot down ideas
- Pens

Introduction

Today we are going to look at a short text, decide how the behaviour of the characters can be interpreted from different viewpoints and then role-play another scenario.

What is a viewpoint? How someone might see, or feel about, a situation.

What is a scenario? An imagined situation.

Read the text on Resource Sheet 1 as a whole class. Discuss the meanings of any new words.

What are the possible different viewpoints of each character of the incident?
Allow paired talk for a few minutes. An example might be: Gemma is upset that Bradley and she were having a lovely time together and then he just walked off for no reason and without saying he was going.

Who would like to hot-seat as one of the characters to tell us how you are feeling or answer questions about how you are feeling?

What clues are there to show how Gemma/Chloe/Bradley feels?

What gestures and actions can be used to portray the characters' feelings?

Discuss ideas to create scenarios to show how behaviour can be interpreted from different viewpoints.

Explain the activity.

Activity

MIXED ABILITY GROUPS

Display or hand out copies of Resource Sheet 2. Read through together each of the three scenarios. Allow some paired talk about the characters' possible different viewpoints about the incident. Then ask some children to share their ideas with the whole class.

Organise the children into groups of three.

- Each group of three should select (or be given) one of the three possible scenarios on Resource Sheet 2.
- The groups should make up a short sketch to role-play the different viewpoints of each character in the scenario.
- Remind the children that they should use gestures, facial expressions, tone of voice and actions to role-play their character's interpretation of the behaviour to the class.

Teacher and support adult should circulate and support groups as appropriate.

Key Vocabulary

characters, role-play, behaviour, viewpoints, scenarios, interpret, hot-seat, gestures, actions, facial expressions, tone of voice, practising, performing, portray, emotions, feelings, peers

Plenary

Select some groups to perform their play to the class.

Did they manage to create roles showing how behaviour can be interpreted from different viewpoints?

Did they use appropriate gestures, actions, facial expressions and tone of voice?

Two's Company, Three's a Crowd

A excitedly explains to B and C that, as a birthday treat, A is allowed to take two friends to see the latest children's film and then go for a pizza. A asks B and C to go.

B gets really excited too, but C says s/he hates going to the cinema and abruptly walks away.

A is very upset and wishes they hadn't asked C.
B is shocked and can't understand why C was so rude.
C is upset because s/he wants to go but can't because his/her parents disapprove of the cinema (or find your own reason).

A and B are discussing going to the funfair together on Saturday afternoon.
C can't go because s/he is visiting her/his sick grandmother.

On the way to the funfair on Saturday afternoon, A and B see C in the town centre with her/his grandmother.

A is angry that C lied.
B is upset because C doesn't want to be friends with her/him anymore.
C is scared of funfairs since s/he was trapped on a ride, a few years earlier (or find your own reason).

A and B are discussing going bowling. C tells them s/he is busy that day.
A and B ask C why s/he never goes out with them.
C walks off without answering them.

A thinks that C is very rude. B is worried about C – that isn't like her/him to ignore them and walk off.

C is embarrassed because her/his parents only have enough money for essentials and can't afford treats (or find your own reason).

Making Long Vowels Short

Learning Objective

- To spell two-syllable words containing double consonants

Success Criteria

- I can spell two-syllable words containing double consonants.

CD-ROM Resources

- PowerPoint file
- Copies of the differentiated Activity Sheets

Other Resources

- Pens, pencils

Introduction

Today we are going to learn to spell two-syllable words where doubling a consonant makes a long vowel a short one.

What are the vowels? a e i o u

What are vowel digraphs? A combination of vowel graphemes that sound as a single phoneme, such as 'ai', 'ea' and 'oa'.

What is a consonant? Any letter other than a vowel; for example, p, s, t, h.

What is a short vowel? One that uses the letter sound, not its name; for example, a as in *apple*, e as in *egg*.

What is a long vowel? One that says its name; for example, a as in *baby*, i as in *fine*, o as in *cola*.

Write this rule on the board: 'Doubling a consonant makes a long vowel a short one.' Then write the word 'bitter'.

How many consonants – double or single – in the middle of this word? Two.

So is the vowel sound a short one or long one? Short.

Explain that 'bitter' means that something tastes sharp, sour and unpleasant. Eating or drinking something that is bitter, such as a lemon, makes you wince or shudder.

Who can mime the word 'bitter' for us?

Now write 'biter' on the board and repeat the steps used for 'bitter'. Ask volunteers to mime other short vowel words, such as 'comma', 'hopping' and 'tapping' (you might need to whisper the words to them). The others should guess which word it is. Write it on the board and then ask the children to apply the rule to find the long vowel word and write it on the board (coma, hoping and taping). Do the same with other words: dinner, diner, supper, super and so on. Ask the class to show thumbs up if the word is spelled correctly and thumbs down if they think it is not.

Explain the activity.

Activity

AA

These children should make up sentences for each of the words in the following word bank, clearly showing them in context.

Short vowel (letter sound)	Long vowel (letter name)
bitter	biter
comma	coma
dinner	diner
hopping	hoping
supper	super
tapping	taping

For reference, the children can be given the word bank cut from the bottom of Activity Sheet.

Extension: Challenge the children to find out which letters we do not find as double consonants.

MA

These children should complete their sentences by filling in the appropriate missing words from the word bank.

Extension: As for.

LA & SEN

These children should fill in the missing letters to complete the words in the sentences, using the correct spelling of the word as in the word bank. **Support as required.**

Extension: As for.

Key Vocabulary

vowel, consonant, long vowel, short vowel

Plenary

Which type of vowel is followed by double consonants?

Short vowels are followed by double consonants and long vowels are followed by single consonants.

What other words can you think of that contain double consonants?

List them on the board.

Who has found a letter that we don't find as a double consonant?

List them on the board.

Making Long Vowels Short

✱ Complete these sentences. Use the word bank below.
✱ Use the rule to check you have the correct spelling.

1. Lemons taste b_____.

2. The man had been in a c_____ for a month.

3. I am h_____ to go to the cinema tonight.

4. The d_____ in the restaurant ordered spaghetti.

5. The vicious dog was a b_____.

6. "What's for s_____?"

7. The girl wanted spaghetti for d_____.

8. There was someone t_____ on the window.

9. I was h_____ because I hurt my leg.

10. "What a s_____ shirt!"

11. A c_____ separates two adjectives.

12. We were t_____ a film onto DVD.

Short vowel (letter sound)	Long vowel (letter name)
bitter	biter
comma	coma
dinner	diner
hopping	hoping
supper	super
tapping	taping

I can use the double consonants rule to select the correct word. ☐

Mad Mnemonics

Learning Objective

- To develop a range of personal strategies for learning new and irregular words

Success Criteria

- I can use mnemonics as a strategy to help me spell new or irregular words.

CD-ROM Resources

- PowerPoint file
- Copies of the Activity Sheet

Other Resources

- The children's literacy books
- Whiteboards and pens
- Lined paper
- Pens
- Dictionaries

Introduction

Today we are going to look at mnemonics and how we can use them as a strategy for learning to spell new and irregular words.

Does anyone know what a mnemonic is?
A formula or aid to assist the memory.

Explain that the spelling of some words is difficult for us to remember. Using a mnemonic is a good way of remembering the spelling, and it's fun too!

Who can spell 'believe' for me?

Write on the board:
believe
Blue elephants lived in early Victorian England.

Explain that the funnier they are, the better, because they are easier to remember, but they have to make some sense.

Write on the board:
pencil
Puppies eat noodles cooked in lemonade.

Write on the board:
wear (to wear clothes)
Waxy ears are revolting.

Can you think of another mnemonic for 'wear'?
Give the children two minutes to talk with the person sitting next to them. Then ask some children to share their mnemonics with the class.

Write any particularly good ones on the board.

Explain the activity.

Activity

Differentiation is primarily dependent on individual children's previous spelling mistakes.

ALL GROUPS
Individually or in pairs, according to ability, the children should check through their literacy books for spelling mistakes they have made. They should then write some good mnemonics for them.

They should practise on whiteboards first, and then write them on lined paper once they are happy with them.

After they have made up their mnemonics, they could test them out with a partner (if they've worked individually) or with another pair (if they've worked in pairs). So, for example, one child might have made up a mnemonic for the word 'witch'. She would then say the mnemonic to her partner, who would have to spell the word.

On the Activity Sheet, the boxes on the left are for the children to record their mnemonics and the section on the right is for them to record what they think their partner's word is after listening to their mnemonic.

Extension: The children could find new and irregular spellings in a dictionary and write mnemonics for them.

Provide support for the LA group where necessary.

Key Vocabulary

spelling, mnemonic, strategy

Plenary

Share some of the mnemonics from a selection of ability groups.

Ask the class to test the mnemonics on their whiteboard to see how successful they are as a strategy to help them spell.

Could you use the mnemonic to spell this word?

Explain to the children that what works for one person may not work for another.

Mad Mnemonics

My Mnemonics

Word _____	Word _____
Mnemonic	Mnemonic
Word _____	Word _____
Mnemonic	Mnemonic
Word _____	Word _____
Mnemonic	Mnemonic

My partner's words

I can use mnemonics as a strategy to help me spell new or irregular words. ☐

Learning Objective

- To write a new poem based on one read

Success Criteria

- I can write new verses for 'Secret Hiding Place'.

CD-ROM Resources

- PowerPoint file
- Slide 3 in the PowerPoint file or copies of the poem (Resource Sheet) to share
- Copies of the differentiated Activity Sheets

Other Resources

- Pens
- Dictionaries
- Thesauruses
- Rhyming dictionaries

Introduction

Today we are going to write poems based on one we will read together.

Read 'Secret Hiding Place' (Resource Sheet) as a whole class.

What is the poem about? Describing the senses.

What are the five senses? Touch, smell, taste, sight, hearing.

What is the pattern of the poem? A B C B

Look at the rhythm, clapping it out together.

Can you identify the pairs of rhyming words in the poem?
Love, above; rainbow, snow; sweet, treat; dear, near.

Ask the children to talk in pairs for a couple of minutes for ideas of what to put into their own 'Secret Hiding Place' poem.

As a whole class, share ideas and mind-map them on the board.

Model writing another verse, asking the children:

Is the rhythm correct?
Have I kept to the ABCB pattern?
Have I used the senses?

Explain to the children that sometimes a line just won't work and you have to start again.

Encourage them to use dictionaries, thesauruses and rhyming dictionaries, if available.

Explain the activity.

Activity

AA
Individually, keeping to the rhyming pattern, these children should write an additional verse for the poem, on their sheet, and then their own version of the last verse in rhyme.

MA
Individually, keeping to the rhyming pattern, these children should write two additional verses for the poem, using the existing first and last verse.

LA & SEN
If they are able, these children should write one rhyming verse of their own. Otherwise, they should try to write a non-rhyming verse. Let them work individually, in pairs or in a group. **Provide support as necessary.**

The teacher should circulate and help children where needed, reading out any good verses as exemplars to the class.

Key Vocabulary

poem, pattern, rhyme pattern, rhythm, rhyming, line, verse, thesaurus, dictionary, version, perform

Plenary

Select children from different ability groups to recite their poems to the class.

Evaluate the writing.

Is the rhythm correct?

Have they kept to the ABCB pattern?

Have they used the senses?

Secret Hiding Place

I have a secret hiding place
For all the things I love,
From the ground beneath my feet
Up to the stars above.

The smell of fresh baked bread,
Bright colours of the rainbow,
The sound of children laughing
And the feel of cold, wet snow.

The sight of my dog's tail wagging,
The taste of my favourite sweet,
The warmth of my mum's tightest cuddle
And the surprise of a birthday treat.

It's full of precious memories
Of which I hold so dear.
So if ever I feel sad and blue
I always have it near.

CANDY ADLER AND KATIE COLLINS

Learning Objective

- To compare materials on the basis of their properties, relating them to their everyday use

Success Criteria

- I can investigate what materials my clothes are made from.

CD-ROM Resources

- PowerPoint file
- Slide 5 in the PowerPoint file or an enlarged copy of Resource Sheet 1
- Copies of Resource Sheet 2, cut in two
- Slide 9 in the PowerPoint file or an enlarged copy of Answers Sheet

Other Resources

- Paper
- Pens and pencils

Introduction

Today we are going to investigate what materials our clothes are made from and think about why these materials might have been used.

Explain that some materials are naturally occurring, such as wool from sheep and cotton from plants. But others, such as polyester and acrylic, are made by people (manufactured).

What material do you think my shirt/blouse is made from? Normally polyester, cotton, a polyester cotton mix or acrylic. *Why do you think it is made from this material and not paper?*

The jumper? Possibly polyester, acrylic, wool or a mixture. *Why isn't it made from plastic?*

The trousers/skirt? Possibly wool, polyester, cotton, polyester and cotton mixed or acrylic.

Shoes? Leather uppers, canvas (thick, heavy cotton). Imitation leather is made from vinyl, vinyl coated fabric or plastic. Soles are usually rubber or leather. *Why do you think my shoes are made from leather and rubber and not cotton?*

Socks? Often acrylic, nylon, polyester or cotton, or a mixture (used to be 100% sheep wool). *What other material could they be made from?*

Display the Venn diagram (Resource Sheet 1) and ask volunteers to sort the materials into manufactured and natural fibres, by writing them into the correct sections.

Why do you think the circles overlap? What could be written in the overlapping part?

Explain that sometimes an item could belong in both circles and so should be written in the overlapping part of the diagram. For example, buttons are usually made from plastic or metal but are sometimes covered in a material to match the item of clothing.

Why do you think that our clothing is made from a mixture of natural and manufactured fibres? They might be harder wearing or easier/cheaper to source/make.

Explain the activity.

Activity

IN ABILITY GROUPS
The children should:
- help each other to find the labels inside their clothes – not undergarments;
- consider what material their zips, buttons, elastic and soles of shoes may be made from;
- use the Word Banks provided (Resource Sheet 2) to help them. This can be left on display or printed out and cut up for the children to use.

AA
Independently, these children should draw themselves in their clothes. They should then label each item of clothing, stating the materials that each is made from, whether it is natural or manufactured and what properties each material has that makes it appropriate (for example, cotton shirt: light, flexible, easily washable).

MA
Independently, these children should also draw themselves in their clothes. They should then label each item of clothing, stating the materials that each is made from and whether it is natural or manufactured.

LA & **SEN**
Independently, these children should also draw themselves in their clothes. They should then label each item of clothing and name the materials that each is made from. **Give support as required.**

Key Vocabulary

materials, manufactured, natural, fibres, properties, wool, leather, nylon, cotton, polyester, silk, acrylic, rubber, vinyl, plastic, imitation leather, canvas, metal

Plenary

What materials are your clothes made from? Choose a couple of the children's pictures to discuss.

Why do you think it is made from that material?

What properties does it have that makes this material suitable for a …?

What would happen if it were made from paper/glass/plastic?

What other material could it be made from instead?

Why do you think manufactured materials were invented?

Display the Answers Sheet and ask volunteer children to sort any new materials and write their names in the correct section.

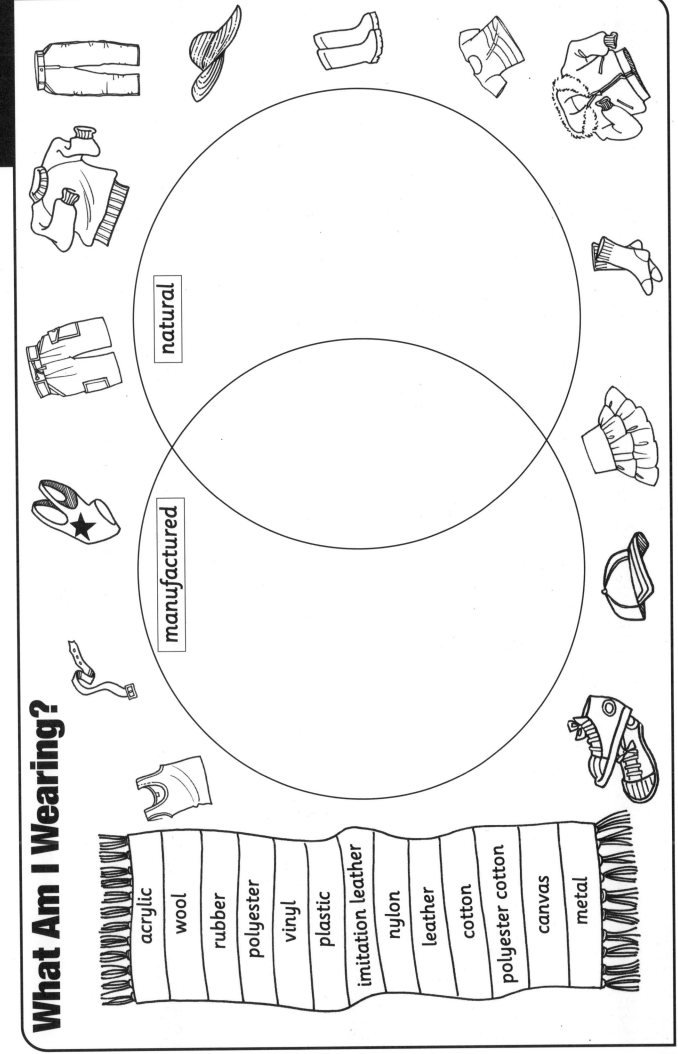

What Am I Wearing?

natural

manufactured

acrylic · wool · rubber · polyester · vinyl · plastic · imitation leather · nylon · leather · cotton · polyester cotton · canvas · metal

Design a Savannah Grassland Animal

Learning Objectives	Introduction	Activity	Plenary
• To find out about some of the animals that live in an African savannah grassland • To design a new species of animal to live in an African savannah grassland	*Today we are going to be explorers and discover a new species of animal, like nothing ever seen before, whose characteristics are completely suited to the savannah grasslands.* **What is a habitat?** The natural home of an animal or plant. That habitat should provide the plant or animal with everything it needs in order to survive. It will provide the food, water and shelter they need, and somewhere to breed.	**AA** These children should design and name an animal they have 'discovered' in the savannah grassland. They should produce an information sheet explaining its features and characteristics, as shown on Resource Sheet 2. **Extension:** They could produce a food chain (Plant → Prey → Predator) for their animal.	Share some of the children's work, evaluating the features of their designs for suitability to the habitat. *Are its features adapted to the environment in which it lives?* *What about its colouring – will it act as camouflage from predators?* *Do you think your new species of animal will be able to withstand the extreme weather changes?*
Success Criteria	**What is a savannah grassland?** A hot, dry grassy environment with scattered trees. It has a very long dry season and a rainy season.	**MA** These children should design and name an animal they have 'discovered'in the savannah grassland. A full description of its characteristics and features must be given, together with a labelled picture of what it might eat. **Extension:** They could illustrate a possible predator of their animal.	
• I can design a new species of animal to live in an African savannah grassland. **CD-ROM Resources**	**Where are savannahs?** Savannahs are located in Africa, Madagascar (an island off the east coast of Africa), Australia, South America, India, and the Myanmar–Thailand region of Southeast Asia. **What sort of animals live in an African savannah?** Display Resource Sheet 1: warthog, giraffe, elephant and cheetah. Discuss the variations of their features to suit their individual habitats within the savannah grasslands, and their feeding habits.	**LA & SEN** These children should design and name an animal they have 'discovered' in the savannah grassland. Each characteristic and feature should be labelled. **Support as required.** **Extension:** They could draw a picture of what it might eat and label it.	
• PowerPoint file • Slide 4 in the PowerPoint file or an enlarged copy of Resource Sheet 1 • Slide 5 in the PowerPoint file or an enlarged copy of Resource Sheet 2 • Copies of Resource Sheet 2	Display Resource Sheet 2 and read together the information on each animal. Reinforce that the animals' features are adapted to their environment.	**Key Vocabulary**	
Other Resources	**What is a herbivore?** Plant-eater. **What is a carnivore?** Meat-eater.	**animal, savannah grassland, habitat, plant, survival, food, water, shelter, breed, season, warthog, giraffe, savannah elephant, cheetah, feeding habits, herbivore, carnivore, prey, predator, food chain, suitability, features, limbs, environment, adapted, suited, camouflage**	
• Paper • Pens, pencils and crayons	Remind the children of the conditions of a grassland savannah – dry, hot, not much water, grasses and scattered trees; although during rainy seasons it is waterlogged and not as hot. Explain the activity.		

Savannah Grassland Animals

Warthog

Description:
- Wild member of pig family
- Almost hairless except for some long bristles
- Name comes from large warts on flat head, which are used as weapons by males
- Two pairs of curved tusks stick out from mouth; used for digging and fighting
- Tuft of hair at end of thin tail
- Can be up to 1.5m long and weigh up to 150kg
- Kneels on front knees to dig for food

Habitat: Open woodland savannah, around water holes and marshy areas

Diet: Omnivore – mainly grass and roots, but also bulbs, berries, insects, worms and bones

Savannah Elephant

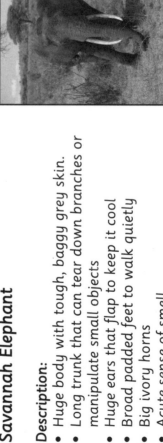

Description:
- Huge body with tough, baggy grey skin.
- Long trunk that can tear down branches or manipulate small objects
- Huge ears that flap to keep it cool
- Broad padded feet to walk quietly
- Big ivory horns
- Acute sense of smell
- Tail used to swat flies

Habitat: Finds shade in a forest or water in hottest part of the day

Diet: Herbivore – leaves, fruit, bark, grass and herbs

Giraffe

Description:
- Tallest land animal
- Long neck enables it to eat from the tops of trees and see predators coming
- Can run up to 35mph/56kph to avoid predators (cheetahs, lions)
- Tough lips and thick saliva enables it to eat thorns
- Back legs slightly shorter than front
- Beige or orangey colour with brown 'splodges' as camouflage
- Short horns on top of head

Habitat: Dry, open wooded areas (sleeps standing up)

Diet: Herbivore – leaves, twigs and bark from the tops of the thorny acacia plant. Can go for days without water. Has to spread front legs and bend long neck to the water

Cheetah

Description:
- Fastest land animal
- Can run up to 65mph/100kph
- Long legs for speed
- Adult male up to 2.25m long
- Yellowish-brown with black spots and 'tear' lines from eyes to mouth as camouflage
- Chases prey, knocks to ground and kills by biting neck
- Long tail to help make quick turns during the chase

Habitat: Dry bushes, open grass, scrub and open forests

Diet: Carnivore – young giraffes, impalas, gazelles and other small hoofed animals

Taking a Line For a Walk

Learning Objective	Introduction	Activity	Plenary
• To explore the use of line to create a pattern using a pencil, in the style of Paul Klee	**Today we are going to look at a painting done by the artist Paul Friedlander, which he did in the style of another, more famous artist, Paul Klee. We are then going to create our own version.**	**ALL ABILITIES**	Share some of the children's pictures and ask the class to evaluate them.

Does the pattern look considered and not scribbled?

Are the colours bright and contrasting?

Is the colouring neat and even?

Could it be improved? |

| **Success Criteria** | Display the painting (Resource Sheet).

How do you think the artist made this pattern?

The technique is called 'Taking a line for a walk', for which Paul Klee is well known. It looks as if the artist has put the point of a pencil on the page and just wandered all over the page with it. Explain that it is good to be creative in an unplanned way. | • All the children should 'take a line for a walk', using the A4 paper horizontally.
• They should think of something they like (happy thoughts), to inspire them while they are working.
• Lines are to be drawn slowly, in a considered way, as if ambling along, looking around as they go.
• Lines should preferably be curved movements rather than straight.
• The children should consider the colours the artist has used and use this style of contrasting colours to colour their own artwork. | |
| • I can explore the use of line to create a pattern using a pencil, in the style of Paul Klee. | | | |

| **CD-ROM Resources** | **What shapes can you identify in his picture?**
Many irregular polygons (three or more sided, closed shapes) and some parts of circles. Point out that some shapes are repeated and they all overlap each other.

What do you notice about the texture?
It is patterned in some areas.

What do you notice about the colour?
It is very bright with a wide range of colours. | • Their artwork must be coloured in even strokes of colour, remaining within the lines drawn.
• Their artwork does not have to have texture.
• The children should evaluate their own work, and then ask others to evaluate it.

Have I used even strokes?
How can I improve it?
Have I coloured it in with care?

Support where appropriate. | |
| • PowerPoint file
• Slide 3 in the PowerPoint file or an enlarged version of the Resource Sheet | | | |

| **Other Resources** | Tell the children a bit about Paul Klee:
Paul Klee was born in 1879 in Switzerland but lived in Germany for a long time, where he studied art at the Munich Academy of Fine Art. He taught and wrote about art, as well as painting. He returned to Switzerland and became ill with a rare disease. He died in 1940.

Explain the activity.

Stress that it is not scribble you are looking for, rather a considered, slow forming of the lines. Colouring in must be of a high standard. If using felt-tipped pens, the children must colour in strokes, in one direction only; otherwise the result will be very uneven and patchy. | **Extension:** Instead of curved movements, take a line for a walk in rectangular movements like a street map with lots of right angles, calling it 'A Walk Around The Block'.

Key Vocabulary
Paul Klee, artist, explore, line, create, pattern, forming, circular movements, overlapping, repeated shapes, colour, contrasting, texture | |
| • A4 paper
• Pencils
• Coloured pencils or felt-tipped pens | | | |

Taking a Line For a Walk

Image by Paul Friedlander www.paulfriedlander.com

Learning Objectives

- To understand the use and importance of map symbols
- To design some simple map symbols

Success Criteria

- I understand the use and importance of map symbols.
- I can design simple map symbols.

CD-ROM Resources

- PowerPoint file
- Slide 4 in the PowerPoint file or an enlarged copy of Resource Sheet 1
- Slide 6 in the PowerPoint file or an enlarged copy of Resource Sheet 2
- Copies of the Activity Sheet

Other Resources

- Coloured pencils
- Blank paper to practise designs

Introduction

Today we are going to look at the purpose of map symbols and design some of our own.

What are maps and what do we use them for? 2D representation of our 3D world; many everyday uses: e.g. travel (to find out how to get from A to B); weather; overview of world (atlas, globe); and so on.

Can anyone tell me what a map symbol is? A representation of an object on the ground.

Why is it useful to have symbols on maps? Enables information to be conveyed visually in a small amount of space.

Display the symbols on Resource Sheet 1.

If these were on a map, what do you think they would mean? Facility has wheelchair access; toilets.

Draw a very simple symbol, such as a tent. Ask the children what it might be and what it might represent on a map (campsite). Point out that the drawing is really simple and that is what makes it effective.

What does every map need to show what the symbols mean? A key.

Display Resource Sheet 2. Talk about how this map is not easy to use – i.e. cluttered and confusing labels.

What would make this map easier to read? The use of symbols.

Leave Resource Sheet 2 on display for the children to refer to during the activity.

Explain the activity.

Activity

ALL ABILITY GROUPS
Differentiation by outcome.

Give each child a copy of the Activity Sheet (with blank map and key box). Explain that they should reproduce the map on display, but use symbols that they will design, rather than the text labels. The children should work independently (or in pairs if appropriate), to design simple map symbols to represent the following: woods, parking area, church, railway station, restaurant, tennis courts, playground, leisure centre.

Using the labelled map on Resource Sheet 2 for reference, the children should place their symbols in the blank map outline, in the position indicated by the appropriate label on the map. Emphasise that the children need to complete a key for their map. **Support where appropriate.**

Extension
The children could use the back of their activity sheet to design further symbols to represent places of interest that they would like to find on their map if it was their ideal place.

Key Vocabulary

map, symbol, information, key, 2-dimensional, 3-dimensional, representation

Plenary

Play 'Guess My Symbol'.

Select one child to draw one of their symbol designs on the board.

What is the symbol representing?

The rest of the class must try to guess which symbol it is.

Repeat with different children.

If any of the children have completed the extension activity, invite some of them to draw their additional symbols and ask the others to guess what they are.

Map Symbols

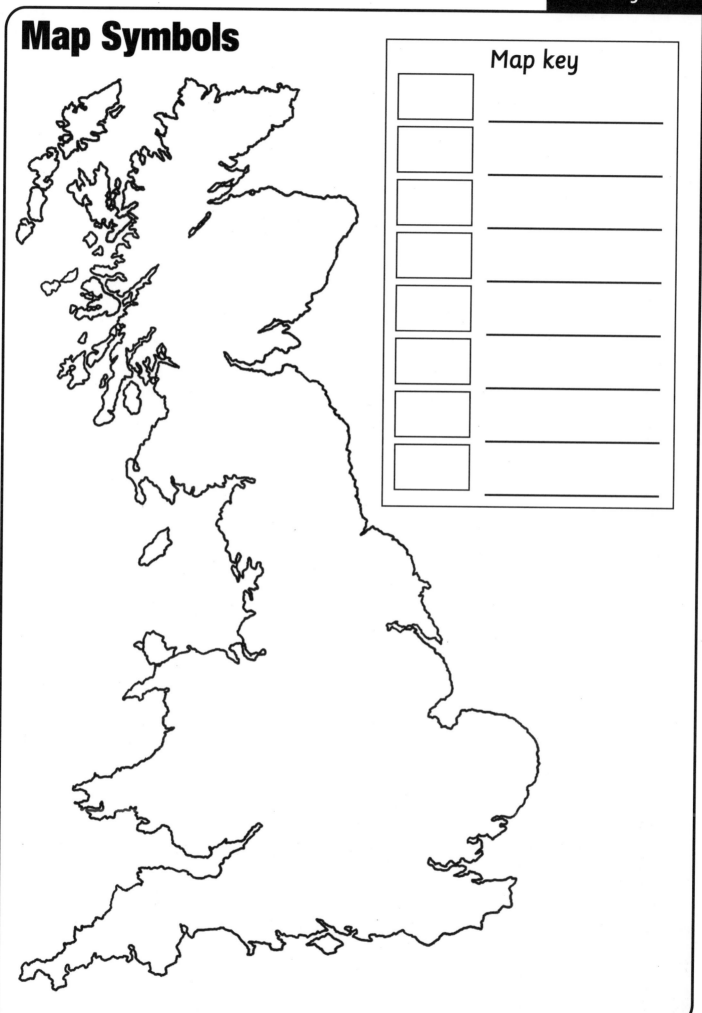

Map key

Censored!

Learning Objective	Introduction	Activity	Plenary
• To know about people's experiences of censorship during the Second World War	**Today we are going to learn about the censorship of letters to and from the troops in WWII, and then censor a letter.** **What does censorship mean?** Control or restriction.	**IN ABILITY GROUPS OF 4** The groups of children should work together as a censorship unit. They should read through their letter (the differentiated Activity Sheets) and discuss what words, phrases, sentences or paragraphs should be 'blue-pencilled'. They can use the mind-map of bombing targets on the board, the mind-map they produced of sensitive language and the Vocabulary Bank (Resource Sheet 2) to help them. When they have agreed on a word or phrase they think should be censored, each child should underline it in pencil on their individual copy of the letter. They continue to work through the letter in this manner until censorship is complete.	Show the children the blue-pencilled copy of the letter (Resource Sheet 3). Show them the blacked out version first. Explain that this is the full version of the letter Gunner Albert Williams would see. Ask the children to look at how little of the letter is actually left to read. Read it out loud.

Success Criteria

	Introduction (cont.)	Activity (cont.)	Plenary (cont.)
• I can use my knowledge about people's experience of censorship during the Second World War to censor a letter.	Explain that letters to and from the Armed Forces (troops including Army, Navy and Royal Air Force) were censored, and any information that might be useful to the enemy was blacked out. This was also called 'blue-pencilled'. Words, phrases, sentences and sometimes whole paragraphs were crossed through in blue or black pencil. Each censorship unit had its own stamp and number. Show the children the coloured envelope (Resource Sheet 1). **Why do you think there is more than one unit stamp?** Usually there are two; letters were read once in the field (wherever the forces were) and once at home. This envelope shows that the letter inside was censored once in the field but twice by the same unit in Britain – this is probably because the unit commander was checking it was done properly.	**AA** 📇 These children should work on the full version of the letter. **MA** 📇 These children should work on the slightly shorter version of the letter. **LA** 📇 **& SEN** These children should work on the adapted version of the letter. **Supported.** **Extension for all ability groups** Design a censorship stamp and give the unit a number. When a final design is decided on, the children may add it to the actual letter.	*How would you feel if you received a letter like this from your loved one?* Then show the class the underlined version of the letter, so they can see what was cut out. Work through the letter as a whole class. *Does everyone agree with blue-pencilling this word/these words?* Explain that lack of agreement was a problem with these units. There were so many of them and so many letters! Some of the units were very meticulous and some of them appeared to be very slapdash. *Can you think of a reason for this difference?*

CD-ROM Resources

* PowerPoint file
* Slide 4 in the PowerPoint file or an enlarged copy of Resource Sheet 1
* Copies of the differentiated Activity Sheets
* Copies of Resource Sheet 2
* Slide 8 in the PowerPoint file or an enlarged copy of Resource Sheet 3

Why do you think it was necessary to censor letters?
It was not safe to write about anything that could be used to build up a picture of life in Britain at war, or give information that might help the enemy to make maps for bombing and invasion. Remember, communication was very different from nowadays. They didn't have computers, the Internet and email. News of the war on the radio, in newspapers or at the cinema was highly censored.

What sort of places would the enemy want to bomb?
Mind-map ideas on the board. Railways and bridges – to immobilise troops and supplies (stop them being transported), airstrips and airports, forces' bases, ports, harbours, factories (especially steelworks, aircraft, ammunition, car manufacturers), London (because it is a capital city and the government is based there), gun placements and so on.

What sort of language would be censored? In groups, on A2 sugar-paper, mind-map (using the information on mind-mapped places the board), for three minutes.

Give out, read together and discuss the Vocabulary Bank (Resource Sheet 2) and the 📇 letter. Explain the activity.

Key Vocabulary

World War II, Second World War, the forces, soldier, troops, overseas, airmail letter, censor, censorship, censored (See Resource Sheet 2)

Other Resources

* Pencils
* Whiteboards and pens
* A2 sugar paper
* Marker pens

Censored!

To: Gunner Albert Williams, 139th Jungle Field Regiment, Burma, Royal Army

My dearest Albert,

I miss you so very much, but I am glad you are well, even if you are suffering from the heat over there. Anyway, to cheer you up, I have lots of news from here in Portsmouth. As you know, Doris married our dear son, Bertie last Tuesday. Bertie was given two days leave from the RAF (I'm sure the Forces won't miss one pilot) and Doris was given leave from the Land Army, digging for victory, to come down to Portsmouth. It took her hours to get through the Home Guard at the docks, especially after they took a direct hit last week!

As Donald couldn't get leave from the Navy (he is stationed in France at the moment), Dorothy stood in as best man. She caught the train from Hatfield and it took 4 hours longer than usual because a barrage balloon had come down over the railway tracks at Kings Cross. She said that the gun placement was busy as she neared here – must have been low-flying enemy aircraft on their way to blitz London again. Poor things!

Betty has joined the ATS as a driver, and is off to India to get used to the heat, ready for Burma. I wonder if she'll bump into Larry over there. He's with the 105th Parachute Regiment, as you know. Keep an eye out for them.

Do you remember little Tommy from next door? He's all grown up now and off to Yorkshire for his radar training next week. He doesn't know where he'll be stationed after that, but he's hoping for a submarine.

Everyone sends their love from Portsmouth.

Your loving wife,

Margery

I can censor a letter, using my knowledge of censorship during WWII. ☐

Timelines

Learning Objective

- To place events in chronological order using a timeline

Success Criteria

- I can place the main events of my life on a timeline, in chronological (time and sequence) order.

CD-ROM Resources

- PowerPoint file
- Slides 3, 4 and 5 in the PowerPoint file or enlarged copies of Resource Sheets 1 and 2 (Vertical and Horizontal Timelines)

Other Resources

- A3 paper for children to draw their own timelines
- Pencils, pens

Introduction

Today we are going to look at timelines as a way of ordering dates and events. We are then going to draw a timeline of the major events in our own lives.

Show the enlarged copy of the vertical timeline 'The Anglo-Saxons in Britain' (Resource Sheet 1). Explain that it is an easy reference to key events in the Anglo-Saxon period in British history. Explain that the events are sequenced in chronological order.

What does that mean? In the time and sequence in which the events took place, beginning with the earliest.

Can you identify what event took place immediately after the Vikings attacked Lindisfarne? Alfred becomes King of Wessex.

When did the Romans leave Britain? 410.
Was this before or after King Offa's Dyke was built? Before.
What year was the Battle of Hastings? 1066.
Was this before or after the end of the Roman rule? After.
Why might it be useful to have this information in a timeline? It provides an at-a-glance visual summary of facts.

Now show the enlarged copy of the horizontal timeline 'Henry VIII's Six Wives' (Resource Sheet 2) and discuss what key events it is depicting.

Apart from the subject matter, what is the difference between this and the other timeline?
This is displayed horizontally, the other vertically.

What events could we include in a timeline of our own lives?

Brainstorm and write up on the board, e.g. Birth date, first tooth, beginning nursery, baby brother or sister born, first day of school, first haircut, memorable holiday, and so on.

Explain the activity and demonstrate making a simple timeline based, perhaps, on the first 10 years of your own life.

Activity

The children are to think of the main events of their own lives, using the brainstormed ideas on the board, and any other memorable personal events. They should then make their own timeline, choosing whichever format they (i.e. either vertical or horizontal).

Emphasise to the children that the dates have to be placed on the timeline in chronological order (in the time sequence in which they occurred) beginning with the earliest.

AA
These children should be encouraged to use as exact dates as possible and to design their timeline in proportion to the dates of the events chosen. So, for example, if two events occur close to each other, they should be close together on the timeline line.

MA
Instead of exact dates or even years, these children could use ages to date the events – e.g. 1 year old: walked; 5 years old: started school.

LA & SEN
As for, but instead of writing the event, they could draw a small picture to represent it.
With support as appropriate.

Key Vocabulary

chronological order, timeline, vertical, horizontal, before, after, past, time, sequence, events, dates, earlier, later, century, decade

Plenary

Share a selection of the children's timelines.

Did most timelines depict the same events? What were some of the more unusual events?

What format was the most popular (vertical or horizontal)? Why?

Discuss time vocabulary.

What does decade mean?

Who knows what BC, BCE, AD and CE mean?
Before Christ, Before the Common Era (used in multicultural societies), AD (Anno Domini, after the birth of Christ) and CE (Common Era).

Explain to the children that the 19th century = the 1800s

So, which century are these dates in: 1973? 1793? 1397?

A Vertical Timeline: The Anglo-Saxons in Britain

250 — Anglo-Saxons begin raids on Britain's shores

410 — Romans leave Britain's shores

450 — Anglo-Saxons start settling in Britain

597 — St Augustine is sent by the Pope to bring Christianity to Britain

600 — Seven Anglo-Saxon kingdoms are created across Britain

601 — St Augustine becomes first Archbishop of Canterbury

730 — The Venerable Bede writes history of English people and church

757 — King Offa's Dyke built along the Welsh border

800 — Vikings attack Lindisfarne

871 — Alfred becomes King of Wessex

954 — Vikings defeated at York

1016 — Canute becomes King of England

1066 — King Harold defeated at Battle of Hastings; beginning of Norman rule

Design a Stained-Glass Window

Learning Objectives

- To use a variety of methods and approaches to communicate observations and ideas
- To design a stained-glass window to given criteria

Success Criteria

- I can design a stained-glass window to the criteria set.

CD-ROM Resources

- PowerPoint file
- Slide 4 in the PowerPoint file or an enlarged copy of the Activity Sheet
- Slide 5 in the PowerPoint file or an enlarged copy of the Resource Sheet

Other Resources

- A3 paper for design
- A4 paper for the drawing of the end product
- Pencils, coloured pencils or felt-tipped pens

Introduction

Today we are going to design a stained-glass window.

Explain to the children that there is to be a new (fictional) Ministry for Child Wellbeing. ('Ministry' means a government department. 'Wellbeing' means health and happiness.) The Ministry wants a stained-glass window to be designed to complement their motto, 'All Children Matter'. The design brief is to illustrate children's needs. Show them the Activity Sheet.

What does 'needs' mean?
Things that are necessary for survival.

What needs do all children have?
Elicit from the children: food, shelter, water, heat, light, love and education. Write them on the board. Remind them that a new designer sweatshirt or trainers, mobile phone top-up and so on are wants, not needs!

Show them the pictures of the stained-glass windows on the Resource Sheet and discuss them. Explain that stained-glass windows are made from pieces of richly coloured glass, which are placed together, similar to a mosaic or jigsaw, to make a picture. Between each piece of glass is a strip of lead to secure the pieces of glass together (these days copper is sometimes used, as it is more flexible).

Remind the children of the design brief (above) and a child's needs: food, shelter, water, heat, light, love and education.

How can you represent these needs in a picture?
Perhaps bread for food and a glass for water.

Explain the activity.

Tell the children that simple drawings and representations will probably work best. Their window may be any shape or style they like, but must be planned in detail and labelled. Encourage them to experiment with different shapes and designs using sketches before they produce their final design.

Activity

Children work individually. Differentiation is by outcome.
The Activity Sheet should be used for the initial planning of the window. This might include the shape of window chosen, suggestions for images and colours, and basic sketches. More advanced planning can be done on A3 paper.

The children should experiment with shapes and designs by sketching and labelling. Each sketch is to be evaluated according to the criteria (conditions) set.

When the final design is decided on, they should produce it on A4 paper with care and attention to detail. The designs must be labelled and details of materials that are to be used should be included.

Once completed, the children should evaluate their own work.

Does it fulfil all the requirements?

How can I improve it?

Extensions
and children could decide on a realistic size for the window and add this to their design sheet.

children could write a short rationale for their choice of shape and the illustrations used.

Key Vocabulary

design, design process, features, materials, components, requirements, experiment, design brief, sketching, labelling

Plenary

Select children to share their designs and their own evaluation of what they've done.

How can we improve it?

Does it contain all the children's needs?

Ask the class to evaluate each one using one positive comment and one constructive criticism.

Design a Stained-Glass Window

**The Ministry of
Child Wellbeing**

DESIGN BRIEF

You are invited to design a stained-glass window for our new building.

The window may be any shape, style or size but must represent a child's needs:

- water
- food
- heat
- light
- shelter
- love
- education

Musical Moods

Learning Objective

- To listen to, and compare and contrast the atmosphere and mood of two different pieces of music

Success Criteria

- I can consider and compare how composers create moods with their music, by using different elements.

CD-ROM Resources

- PowerPoint file
- Slide 6 in the PowerPoint file or an enlarged copy of the Resource Sheet
- Copies of the Activity Sheet
- Copy of the Teacher Support Sheet
- Audio file of Glenn Miller's 'Pennsylvania 6–5000'
- Audio file of Kenny G's 'Three of a Kind'

Other Resources

- A3 paper
- Pens, pencils

Introduction

Today we are going to listen to, and compare and contrast the atmosphere and mood of two different pieces of music.

Explain to the children that music has different genres in the same way that texts do.

Ask them to fold an A3 sheet of paper in half. Tell them you are going to play them some music. On the left half of their paper they should draw or jot down some words in response to the mood created by the track.

Play Glenn Miller's 'Pennsylvania 6-5000'.

How did it make you feel when you were listening to it? What was it in the music that made you feel that way?

Discuss, but bear in mind that taste and interpretation of music is a very individual thing, so there is no wrong or right answer.

Repeat this for Kenny G's 'Three Of A Kind'. The children should write on the other half of the paper.

Were the moods and atmosphere created different? How?

Replay the tracks to enable the children to listen specifically for clues. Explain that the genre of the first track, 'Pennsylvania 6-5000', is swing (also known as a 'big band sound'), performed by The Glenn Miller Band in 1940.

What do you think the Band used for the telephone?

A bicycle bell.

The genre of the second track, 'Three Of A Kind', is smooth jazz, or contemporary jazz, performed by Kenny G in 1986.

Remind/explain some musical terms. Display the Resource Sheet.

tempo – variations in speed

timbre – quality of the sound, such as jerky, joyful, stirring, bracing, soothing

dynamics – variation in volume, usually loud or quiet

structure – how sounds are organised – beginning, middle and end; repetition

ostinato/ostinati (plural) – short rhythmic pattern/s repeated over and over

Explain the activity.

Activity

Individually or in mixed-ability pairs, whichever is preferred, the children should concentrate on the elements featured on the Activity Sheet – genre, tempo, timbre and so on.

Let them listen to the tracks again for each element, completing each section of the sheet when directed by the teacher (after discussion, unless the answer is personal preferences).

When they have completed the sheet for 'Pennsylvania 6-5000', they should then listen to 'Three Of A Kind' and repeat the above activity.

LA & SEN
Support if appropriate.

Plenary

What instruments were played on each track?

List them on the board (see Teacher Support Sheet).

Which instruments do they both have in common?

Saxophone, bass, drums (Kenny G used a drum machine), keyboard (The Glenn Miller Band used a piano).

Ask a few children to tell you which piece they preferred and why. Encourage the others to join in the discussion.

Did you know?

The Glenn Miller Band is actually an orchestra. An orchestra is large group of musicians who play together on various instruments, usually including strings, woodwinds, brass instruments and percussion instruments. A band is a smaller group of musicians playing together.

'Pennsylvania 6-5000' was named after the Hotel Pennsylvania in America, where the band used to perform. It is the hotel's phone number. The vocals are called a 'hook', like an advertising slogan.

All the instruments in 'Three Of A Kind' were played by Kenny G or Preston Glass. The artists recorded playing one instrument at a time, and it was put together at the end.

Key Vocabulary

elements, atmosphere, mood, composer, performers, big band sound, swing, smooth jazz, instruments, orchestra, tempo, timbre, dynamics, structure, ostinato/ostinati

Musical Moods

✳ Listen carefully to each track. Then answer the questions below or fill in the missing words.

PENNSYLVANIA 6–5000 – THE GLENN MILLER BAND

1) The genre of this track is _____ but sometimes it is known as the Big Band Sound.

2) The track begins with _____

3) Describe the tempo of this track. _____
_____

4) What words can you think of to describe the timbre of the track?
_____
_____

THREE OF A KIND – KENNY G

5) The genre of this track is smooth jazz or _____

6) The track begins with a _____
that carries on throughout the track.

7) Describe the tempo of this track. _____
_____

8) What words can you think of to describe the timbre of the track?
_____
_____

9) Which track do you prefer?
_____

10) Give your reasons. _____
_____

I can consider how composers create mood with their music by comparing tracks. ☐

Design a Coat of Arms

Learning Objectives

- To recognise that symbolism is used in everyday life
- To design some personal symbols on a coat of arms

Success Criteria

- I can design a coat of arms to represent myself.

CD-ROM Resources

- PowerPoint file
- Slide 3 in the PowerPoint file or an enlarged copy of Resource Sheet 1
- Slide 4 in the PowerPoint file or an enlarged copy of Resource Sheet 2
- Copies of the Activity Sheet

Other Resources

- Coloured pencils or felt-tipped pens
- Paper to practise on

NB: The final coats of arms look super cut out and stuck onto coloured paper to give a small border for a display.

Introduction

Today we are going to look at signs and symbols around us and then design a coat of arms to represent ourselves.

We see a wide variety of signs every day, such as car badges, instructions to road users, instructions for washing clothes, signs to show different religions and logos on clothing.

Show some examples (see Resource Sheet 1).

What do each of these mean?

Show Resource Sheet 2 with the example of a coat of arms, this one representing the Queen (not officially hers).

What can you tell about this person from the illustrations?

Can you guess who this coat of arms could represent?

Explain to the children that on a coat of arms the symbols are best kept to very simple versions of whatever is being depicted.

What pictures could you use for Cinderella?

Ideas might include: glass slipper, clock set at midnight, wand, pumpkin, crown

What pictures could you use for yourselves?

Remind the children to think of really positive things about themselves. For example:

- being good at, or enjoying, a particular sport
- loving cooking
- being good at painting
- being good at helping or listening to others

Write some of the examples on the board to help children to think of things to represent themselves.

Optional: draw some simple symbols to illustrate some of them.

Explain the activity.

Activity

ALL CHILDREN INDIVIDUALLY

The children should think of things that interest or represent them and make some notes them on paper. They should then draw a very simple symbol to represent each item on the list.

They should then choose four of the symbols that represent them best and seek teacher approval.

In the scroll at the bottom of the blank shield (Activity Sheet), the children should write their first name (and surname initial if more than one shares the same name).

They should then carefully draw the four selected symbols, ensuring that they are fairly large (not a tiny little symbol in the middle of a large section) and then colour them.

LA & SEN
Peer or teacher support, whichever is more appropriate.

Extension: The children could think of someone famous (real or fictitious) who they admire and make a list of things that represent them best.

Key Vocabulary

symbol, symbolism, represent, personal, personality, coat of arms, design, pictures

Plenary

Share some of the children's coats of arms. Ensure you cover the name in the scroll when you show it!

Can you guess what the symbols represent?

Can you guess who this coat of arms represents?

Could they have been improved?

Who can tell us which symbols they chose for a famous person?

Design a Coat of Arms

I can design a coat of arms to represent myself. ☐

Learning Objectives	Introduction	Activity	Plenary
• To explore and create characters in response to the musical elements of 'Spring Allegro' • To improvise freely on their own, with a partner and a small group, bringing the characters to life with dramatic effect using movement	*Today we are going to choreograph and perform some phrases in character to Vivaldi's 'Spring Allegro Concerto'.* *What does choreograph mean?* To compose a sequence of steps and moves for a dance. Explain to the children that dance can also be drama, but using movement and facial expressions instead of words. Warm up by doing gentle stretches using all body parts.	**MIXED ABILITY GROUPS** Ask the children to sit and listen while you play the music again. Ask them to listen to the tempo (speed), timbre (quality – jerky, bracing), dynamics (variation in loudness), pitch (how high and low) and beat of the music.	Tell the children it is time to cool down. Tell them they are going to be cats, basking in the sunshine. *What do cats do when they are basking in the sunshine?* They stretch their bodies right out.
Success Criteria • I can explore the elements of 'Spring' through movement and dance.	Listen to the track from Vivaldi 'Four Seasons'. *What does the music remind you of? What happens in spring?* New life, growth, awakening, skipping, warmth, sunshine, freedom from being stuck indoors and so on.	In their groups, they should combine ideas and movements to produce a short piece of movement that is appropriate to the different elements of the music as well as the season of spring. Remind them to vary their body shape, height, group size and directions within their phrase, while responding and keeping in time with the music when performing.	To prepare for stretching as they are lying down, tell them to stretch both arms up towards the sun; then to go onto tip-toes, stretching their legs, still stretching their arms. Continue giving instructions to stretch different parts of their bodies.
CD-ROM Resources • Audio track from Vivaldi's *Four Seasons*: 'Spring Allegro (1st)'	Model some movements of a child peering out of the window gleefully as they realise the rain has stopped and the sun has come out, or of a flower growing towards the sun.	Ask the groups to perform to the class. The others should evaluate the choreography. **NB – Safety issues** • Remove all jewellery and cover any earrings that cannot be removed.	Now they should roam around the room looking for a good place to lie down, well away from anyone else. Finally let them lie down and pretend to be cats basking in the sunshine.
Other Resources • A CD player or other sound system • A whistle to attract attention	Ask the children to individually improvise the actions of an animal or flower, in time to the music. Remind them to be aware of others. Select some good examples to share as you go round. The children should then repeat the exercise in pairs, combining ideas.	• Wear shoes while walking to and from the hall. • Remind children to be mindful of other people's space when dancing.	Then ask everyone to sit up and listen to you. Remind them of the movements they did to the Vivaldi music. *How effective were your movements?* *How could you change them to improve your choreography?*
	As you observe, ask them to change, vary and develop the actions, space, dynamics and relationships (how partners and groups position themselves), and to look at shape and patterning. Help them to copy and adapt different step patterns and gestures.	**Key Vocabulary** **explore, create, response, improvise freely, choreograph, perform, dramatic effect, movement, stretches, vary, body shape, height, group size, direction, phrase, sequence, actions, space, dynamics, patterning, spring (the season and the action)**	*Did you work well as a group?*

Success Criteria

I can explore the elements of the spring season through movement and dance.

✔ I can think about the elements of spring and explore these through movement and dance, in response to the changes in the music.

✔ I can remember to use my facial expressions, head and hands as well as my limbs.

✔ I can work with my group to produce and perform a short dance phrase to represent spring.

Supply Teacher Feedback Form

Class:

Supply Teacher's Name:

Date:

| **Class behaviour:** (please circle) |

Excellent   **Good**   **Satisfactory**   **Unsatisfactory/Poor**

Incidents:

| **Maths:** |

☺ Excelled:

☹ Struggled:

| **Literacy:** |

☺ Excelled:

☹ Struggled:

| **Other subjects:** |

☺ Excelled:

☹ Struggled:

Other subjects:

☺ Excelled:

☹ Struggled:

| **Additional information/General comments:** |

Signed:

Supply Teacher Feedback Form – Sample

Class: 3A   **Date:** 21/11/2009

Supply Teacher's Name: Candy Adler

Class behaviour: (please circle)

Excellent   (**Good**)   **Satisfactory**   **Unsatisfactory/Poor**

Incidents: Connor and Lewis were both very silly. Separated them.
Kerry seemed to be very sad today.

Maths: To use knowledge of place value up to 3 digits to complete a grid

☺ Excelled: Jordan, Kelly, Henry, Elizabeth, Flynn

☹ Struggled: Connor, Lewis, Kerry, Natalie

Literacy: To understand the term 'collective noun' and collect examples

☺ Excelled: Keiran, Jake, Jordan, Natalie, Harry

☹ Struggled: Connor, Lewis, Kerry, Drew

Other subjects: Art – To explore the use of line to create a pattern using a pencil, in the style of Paul Klee

☺ Excelled: Scott, Kelly, Henry

☹ Struggled: Natalie

Other subjects: History – To place events in chronological order using a timeline

☺ Excelled: Jordan, Kelly, Henry, Elizabeth,

☹ Struggled: Drew, Matthew

Additional information/General comments:

I had a lovely day with your class!

Signed:

Maths

Tables: What's My Question?

Across	
1.	7 x 7
3.	9 x 2, 2 x 9, 6 x 3, 3 x 6
5.	8 x 8
9.	7 x 3, 3 x 7
10.	7 x 5, 5 x 7
11.	9 x 6, 6 x 9
14.	8 x 7, 7 x 8
16.	9 x 9
17.	9 x 4, 6 x 6, 4 x 9
19.	8 x 3, 6 x 4, 4 x 6, 3 x 8
21.	8 x 6, 6 x 8
22.	5 x 3, 3 x 5
24.	10 x 2, 5 x 4, 4 x 5, 2 x 10
25.	7 x 6, 6 x 7
27.	9 x 7, 7 x 9
30.	8 x 2, 4 x 4, 2 x 8
31.	7 x 4, 4 x 7
33.	6 x 5, 10 x 3, 5 x 6, 3 x 10
34.	9 x 3, 3 x 9
36.	6 x 2, 4 x 3, 3 x 4, 2 x 6
38.	9 x 5, 5 x 9
39.	8 x 3, 6 x 4, 4 x 6, 3 x 8
40.	9 x 6, 6 x 9

Down	
1.	7 x 6, 6 x 7
3.	6 x 2, 4 x 3, 3 x 4, 2 x 6
4.	9 x 9
5.	9 x 7, 7 x 9
6.	9 x 5, 5 x 9
7.	9 x 8, 8 x 9
11.	8 x 7, 7 x 8
12.	7 x 4, 4 x 7
13.	9 x 7, 7 x 9
14.	10 x 5, 5 x 10
15.	8 x 3, 6 x 4, 4 x 6, 3 x 8
18.	8 x 8
19.	7 x 4, 4 x 7
20.	8 x 4, 4 x 8
21.	7 x 6, 6 x 7
23.	8 x 7, 7 x 8
25.	8 x 6, 6 x 8
26.	9 x 4, 6 x 6, 4 x 9
28.	8 x 4, 4 x 8
29.	10 x 4, 8 x 5, 5 x 8, 4 x 10
30.	10 x 1, 5 x 2, 2 x 5, 1 x 10
32.	9 x 9
33.	7 x 5, 5 x 7
35.	9 x 8, 8 x 9
37.	5 x 5

Across	
1.	8 x 2, 4 x 4, 2 x 8
2.	7 x 5, 5 x 7
4.	8 x 3, 6 x 4, 4 x 6, 3 x 8
6.	10 x 2, 5 x 4, 4 x 5, 2 x 10
7.	9 x 3, 3 x 9
10.	10 x 3, 6 x 5, 5 x 6, 3 x 10
12.	10 x 2, 5 x 4, 4 x 5, 2 x 10
13.	7 x 3, 3 x 7
15.	8 x 3, 6 x 4, 4 x 6, 3 x 8
17.	7 x 5, 5 x 7
18.	7 x 2, 2 x 7
20.	9 x 6, 6 x 9
21.	8 x 2, 4 x 4, 2 x 8
24.	5 x 2, 2 x 5, 1 x 10
25.	9 x 5, 5 x 9
27.	7 x 2, 2 x 7
28.	8 x 4, 4 x 8
30.	8 x 6, 6 x 8
32.	7 x 4, 4 x 7
33.	3 x 3
34.	4 x 2, 2 x 4

Down	
1.	6 x 2, 4 x 3, 3 x 4, 2 x 6
2.	8 x 4, 4 x 8
3.	10 x 5, 10 x 5
4.	7 x 4, 4 x 7
5.	7 x 2, 2 x 7
7.	10 x 2, 5 x 4, 4 x 5, 2 x 10
8.	6 x 2, 4 x 3, 3 x 4, 2 x 6
9.	7 x 6, 6 x 7
10.	6 x 6
11.	7 x 2, 2 x 7
14.	9 x 2, 6 x 3, 3 x 6, 2 x 9
15.	5 x 5
16.	5 x 3, 3 x 5
17.	6 x 6
19.	10 x 4, 8 x 5, 5 x 8, 4 x 10
21.	6 x 2, 4 x 3, 3 x 4, 2 x 6
22.	10 x 3, 6 x 5, 5 x 6, 3 x 10
23.	9 x 3, 3 x 9
24.	7 x 2, 2 x 7
26.	9 x 6, 6 x 9
27.	9 x 2, 2 x 9
29.	7 x 3, 3 x 7

Maths

Measuring Angles

Answers to

A90° B60° C45° D30° E90° F45° G60° H30° I 180°

1. I   2. D & H   3. A & E   4. I   5. A, B, C, E, F, G, I   6. I, A, E, B, G, C, D, H

Answers to

A=L, B=S, C=S, D=S, E= S, F= B, G=B

Place Value Grids

−1000	−100	−10	−1	Numbers	+1	+10	+100	+1000
5725	6625	6715	6724	6725	6726	6735	6825	7725
3329	4229	4319	4328	4329	4330	4339	4429	5329
234	1134	1224	1233	1234	1235	1244	1334	2234
3160	4060	4150	4159	4160	4161	4170	4260	5160
4000	4900	4990	4999	5000	5001	5010	5100	6000
909	1808	1899	1908	1909	1910	1919	2009	2909
4634	5534	5624	5633	5634	5635	5644	5734	6634
2407	3307	3397	3406	3407	3408	3417	3507	4407
99	999	1089	1098	1099	1100	1109	1199	2099

−100	−10	−1	Numbers	+1	+10	+100
625	715	724	725	726	735	825
229	319	328	329	330	339	429
134	224	233	234	235	244	334
60	150	159	160	161	170	260
790	880	889	890	891	900	990
408	498	507	508	509	518	608
534	624	633	634	635	644	734
307	397	406	407	408	417	507
16	106	115	116	117	126	216

Maths

Place Value Grids (continued)

−10	−1	Numbers	+1	+10	+100
15	24	25	26	35	125
18	27	28	29	38	128
24	33	34	35	44	134
40	49	50	51	60	150
72	61	62	63	72	162
7	16	17	18	27	117
53	62	63	64	73	163
32	41	42	43	52	142
89	98	99	100	109	199

Compass Points Shapes

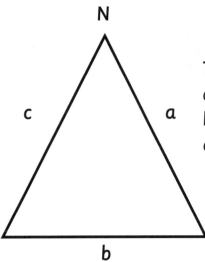

Triangle
a Face SE, 6 steps
b Face W, 4 steps
c Face NE, 6 steps

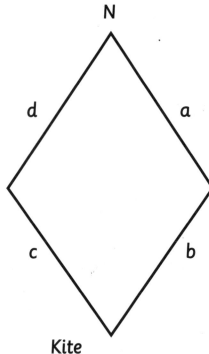

Kite
a Face SE, 4 steps
b Face SW, 4 steps
c Face NW, 4 steps
d Face NE, 4 steps

Rhombus
a Face E, 4 steps
b Face SW, 3 steps
c Face W, 4 steps
d Face NE, 3 steps

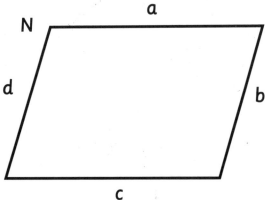

Maths

What's My Name?

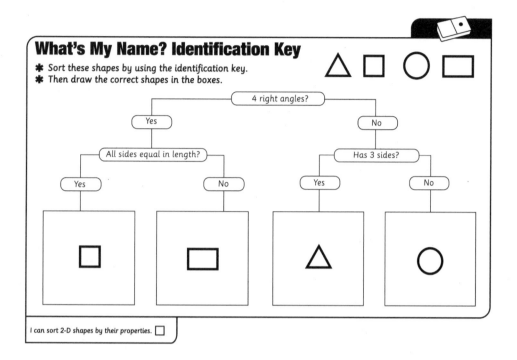

What's My Name? Identification Key

❋ Sort these shapes by using the identification key.
❋ Then draw the correct shapes in the boxes.

I can sort 2-D shapes by their properties. ☐

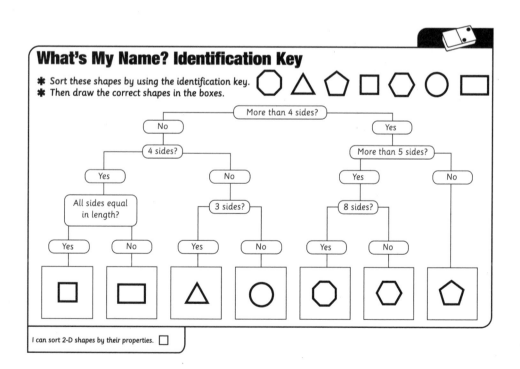

What's My Name? Identification Key

❋ Sort these shapes by using the identification key.
❋ Then draw the correct shapes in the boxes.

I can sort 2-D shapes by their properties. ☐

Literacy

Prefix Perfection Game

un

unstable
unlike
unload
unfair
undo
untidy
unlucky
undress
uncover
unkind
unloved
untrue
unusual
unused
unpick
unhappy
unsafe
unseen
unable
unwell

dis, un

stable – un
like – dis, un
agree – dis
fair – un
read – un
honest – dis
connected – dis, un
lucky – un
obey – dis
please – dis
cover – dis, un
kind – un
trust – dis
armed – dis, un
place – dis
order – dis
used – dis, un
allow – dis
band – dis
happy – un
count – dis
seen – un
qualified – dis, un
just – un
able – dis, un
well – un
comfort – dis
ease – dis, un

mis, dis, un

stable – un
like – dis, un
take – mis
fair – un
read – mis, un
honest – dis
connected – dis, un
informed – mis, un
obey – dis
behave – mis
cover – dis, un
take – mis
trust – mis, dis
fire – mis
place – mis, dis
order – dis
used – mis, dis, un
allow – dis
just – un
hear – mis
count – mis, dis
qualified – dis, un
fit – mis, un
just – un
able – dis, un
well – un
comfort – dis
ease – dis, un

Instant Lessons for Supply Teachers 7–9 Years © A & C Black